Study Guide

Lisa Hager
Spring Hill College

STUDY GUIDE

to accompany

Experiencing The Lifespan

THIRD EDITION

by Janet Belsky

WORTH PUBLISHERS

Study Guide
by Lisa Hager
to accompany
Belsky: *Experiencing the Lifespan*, **Third Edition**

© 2013, 2010, 2007 by Worth Publishers

Printed in the United States of America

ISBN 10: 1-4641-0851-X
ISBN 13: 978-1-4641-0851-8

First Printing

Worth Publishers
41 Madison Ave.
New York, NY 10010
www.worthpublishers.com

CONTENTS

TO THE STUDENT

This **Study Guide** is designed to help you to study effectively and to learn the important concepts in *Experiencing the Lifespan,* Third Edition, by Janet Belsky. Use this study guide in an active manner and as a complement to the textbook, not as a substitute for it. By actively reading the text material and this study guide, you will be able to master the chapter concepts in a straightforward and enjoyable manner. Our goal is to create independent, motivated students who enjoy learning for its own sake, who can think critically, and who have a deep conceptual understanding of the information presented in the text.

Learning about human development is very exciting but it is also challenging. In addition to learning about physical, cognitive, and psychosocial development throughout the lifespan, you will also be learning about research methods, theories of development, genetics, conception, prenatal development, and death and dying. You will be faced with learning new terminology, novel concepts, unfamiliar theories, and practicing your skills at thinking like a scientist. You should find that you are familiar with many of the concepts illustrated in the textbook even if you didn't previously know the proper terminology or theoretical perspective associated with the concept. The author has written the textbook so that it tells a story, is person-centered, hands-on, and emphasizes the application of the material. In the study guide, we have attempted to mirror the textbook author's style by allowing you to take advantage of your prior knowledge of human development. We provide you with opportunities to apply the material from the textbook to your own life and to the lives of those you know. This will aid in your understanding of and memory for the information in the book. Cognitive psychologists refer to this technique as the self-reference effect (Rogers, Kuiper, & Kirker, 1977). When we can use our self-knowledge as retrieval cues for new information, then we are more likely to remember the new information.

How to Use This Guide

Scanning

Scanning is a useful strategy that can facilitate learning. When you scan a chapter, you get a better idea of what lies ahead. So survey the text chapter first. Spend some time looking at the graphics, and examine the special features including "Setting the Context," which offers a cross-cultural perspective, "Interventions," which offers practical applications of the material, "In Focus," which delves more deeply into a topic, and "Experiencing the Lifespan," which are interviews with people of different ages and backgrounds. Note the parts of the chapter that look interesting to you. Pay attention to the diagrams, graphs, photographs, cartoons, and tables. This preview will give you a clearer impression of what is going to be covered in the chapter. Don't worry about the details at this point; just try to get the big picture.

Next read the chapter overview at the beginning of each chapter in the study guide as well as "What It's All About" at the beginning of each major section. This will give you a general, but more detailed summary of what you are about to encounter in the chapter. This type of previewing activity will help you to develop a conceptual framework (or cognitive map) that will allow you to more readily understand the details of what you are about to read and will make learning the material easier. For example, imagine trying to put together a large jigsaw puzzle without knowing what the finished picture looked like. Do you think it would be easier if you could see the finished picture? Of course it would! Likewise, when you scan the chapter and read the preview, you will have some idea of the big picture and of how the various pieces of the chapter fit together.

Chapter Summaries and Outlines

The textbook is divided in six major parts. At the beginning of each new part, the textbook author provides you with a summary of each chapter in that part. At the beginning of each chapter, the textbook author provides an outline of the chapter with the special features (e.g., Interventions) highlighted in the outline. These organizers will help you to start thinking about the material and will give you an overview of what lies ahead. The "Final Thoughts" at the end of each chapter provide a general summary of that chapter as well as a preview to what's coming up in the next chapter.

What You Need to Know and Testing Your Knowledge

For each chapter in the study guide, there are learning objectives listed for each section. These objectives should guide your reading of the chapter and the short-answer and essay questions that follow are designed to test your understanding of the objectives. Most of the questions in these sections ask you to apply the information and demonstrate your understanding of the material. They are not questions that test your ability to memorize a set of facts. Research in psychology has shown that self-generated material, called the Generation Effect, (Slameka & Graf, 1978) enhances our understanding of the material and our ability to remember the material. Why take college courses just to regurgitate facts and forget them afterwards? The approach we have taken is aimed at fostering your understanding and application of the material and not your ability to simply memorize it.

Put It All Together

Each chapter in the study guide has matching, multiple-choice, and short-answer and essay questions. We realize that many instructors may test you using more objective questions and want to give you some practice in applying your understanding of the material to these types of questions. Some of the questions are factually based and others require application. By completing these questions and the textbook questions in the Tying It All Together sections, you should have a good idea of how well you understand the basics of each chapter.

Answer Key

The answer key/guides for the Testing Your Knowledge, Matching Items, Multiple-Choice, and Short-Answer and Essay Questions are at the end of each chapter of this study guide. The questions will be most helpful if you attempt to answer them *before* looking at the answer key/guide. Then look at the items you missed and reread those sections of the textbook to make sure you understand the concepts.

STUDY TIPS

Psychologists have been studying learning and memory for decades. From this research, we have discovered several principles that you can apply to your studying. Here are some tips on how to use the principles.

Use Distributed Practice

You know that you should not cram. Cramming, or what psychologists call massed practice, is not good for long-term retention of material. Spacing out your studying, or distributed practice, on the other hand, enhances your ability to remember. This is one of the most well-established principles in psychology—the spacing effect. Instead of studying for five straight hours at one time, you would be much better off studying one hour a day over five days. This technique also works at shorter intervals. For example, if you have to memorize a formula, you will probably repeat it over and over (say, ten times) until you feel confident you have it memorized. This, of course, is massed practice, and the sense of confidence that typically accompanies it is often misleading. Don't mistake familiarity with knowledge. A better way to maximize the benefits of those ten rehearsals is to space them over time, allowing a longer interval after each rehearsal than the one before.

Reduce Interference

One reason we tend to forget new information is that other information (either previously learned or learned later) can interfere with the material we are trying to master. So, if you are studying for a number of courses at the same time, try to study subjects that are different from each other. The more similar they are, the greater the interference. Another source of interference comes from social activities, such as watching TV or interacting with friends. When you engage in these activities after studying, you increase the risk of interference. In addition, playing loud music, having the TV on, or listening to other people's conversations while you are studying can cause distraction and interfere with learning. The best advice? Go to sleep after studying. A good sleep is the best way to cut down on interference and it helps consolidate memories. The worst thing to do? Stay up all night cramming for an exam that is being given the next day.

Try Overlearning

Overlearning is another very effective, and relatively simple, technique for preventing forgetting. When you feel you have mastered the material in a chapter, and you have just answered all the progress test questions correctly, you usually feel relieved and put away the books. It is at this point, however, that overlearning is useful. If you had spent, say, an hour and a half getting to this level, what you need to do now is spend another 10 to 15 minutes reviewing the material one more time. These few extra minutes of studying are the most beneficial minutes you can spend in terms of consolidating your memory and preventing the forgetting of material you have just learned. Hermann Ebbinghaus showed, over a hundred years ago, that most of the information is lost very soon after it is learned. He was the first to demonstrate the powerful effect of overlearning as a way of dealing with this problem.

Knowing What You Know

If you studied hard and felt you really knew the material, it is a bit of a shock to find that you did poorly on the test. What could have happened? One possibility is that you only thought you knew the material and you were suffering from "the overconfidence effect." A simple way of preventing this is to get corrective feedback on what you know before taking the exam. For example, use the Matching Items, the Multiple-Choice Questions, complete the Testing Your Knowledge and Short-Answer and Essay Questions, and, of course, complete the Tying It All Together sections in the textbook. This will give you the feedback you need. Be aware, however, that this is not necessarily a perfect gauge of how you will do on the real exam. When you are testing yourself, you tend to be in a much more relaxed state. You have just studied the material and you are in no particular rush. If you make a mistake, it is no big deal; you can simply look up the answers at the end of the chapter (this is not something that you can do in the exam!). These factors often lead students to the false conclusion that the questions on the real exam were much harder than the ones in the progress tests, sample exams, and so forth. Try to make your self-testing as real as possible by getting a little anxious and completing the self-testing in an environment that is similar to the classroom. You can try studying in the college or university library, a classroom, or if studying in your room or at home then sit at a desk in a well-lit and quiet environment and don't study while lounging in bed, watching TV, or texting your friends; that way you will benefit most from corrective feedback.

Use Mnemonics

Use of memory aids, called mnemonics, can help in memorizing new material and in preventing forgetting. Visual imagery, in particular, is very effective with some material. Try to vividly imagine what it is you are attempting to memorize. A picture is worth a thousand words and is much more memorable. If the images interact then they can be even more effective. For example, in order to remember that one-year-olds are in Piaget's little scientist stage you might imagine a baby wearing a lab coat and playing with test tubes. For other material, try making up a story that links elements together. Create acronyms for lists of terms or complex concept names, for example (it is easier to remember DABDA than denial, anger, bargaining, depression, and acceptance for Kübler-Ross's stages of accepting death).

Develop Good Study Habits

Most top students get good grades because of effective study habits (not sheer brilliance). Evaluate your current study habits. Do you read the assigned readings before they are covered in class? If so, then take notes from your reading and combine those with notes you take in class. When it's time to study for the test you don't need to reread chapters; you can study your notes instead. As you read, think critically about the information you are reading. Does the author provide objective evidence for the claim? Are the claims supported by correlational or experimental research? Manage your time effectively. Remember, we are usually poor judges about how long things take to do (late papers are a typical example that is the result of our poor judgment). So, after you have made your plans, allow yourself some extra time.

Make studying a priority and firmly commit to doing well in school. Don't let other people interfere with your goal of mastering the material and getting good grades. Study by yourself (too much socializing takes place in study groups). Reward yourself with social activities, if that's what is important to you, AFTER you have successfully completed your study and have achieved an A+ on the progress tests. If you like music, play soft instrumental music. Take a short break after an hour or so of studying—walk around for a few minutes. Do some exercise. Don't study when you are sleep deprived, very tired, or stressed out. If you are getting nowhere and can't concentrate on the material, do something else for a while (a breath of fresh air, a brief nap, a little walk, a chat with a friend, a little meditation or exercise, can all be helpful).

Be a smart test-taker

If a test contains both multiple-choice questions and an essay question, turn first to the essay. Read the question carefully, noting exactly what the instructor is asking. On the back of a page, pencil in a list of points you'd like to make and then organize them. Before writing, put aside the essay and work through the multiple-choice questions. (As you do so, your mind may continue to mull over the essay question. Sometimes the objective questions will bring pertinent thoughts to mind.) Then reread the essay question, rethink your answer, and start writing. When finished, proofread to eliminate spelling and grammatical errors that make you look less competent than you are. When reading multiple-choice questions, don't confuse yourself by trying to imagine how each alternative might be right. Try instead to recall the answer *before* reading the alternatives given. Answer the question as if it were a fill-in-the-blank; first cover the answers and complete the sentence in your mind, and then find the alternative that best matches your own answer (see Myers, *Exploring Psychology in Modules, 9e.* p. 12).

Try Exercise

Exercising before you study will help relieve stress and will induce a more relaxed state. This is because exercise causes the brain to release pain-killing chemicals called endorphins (you have your own little drug-producing factory). It is also a good idea to exercise before a major exam for the same reasons. If aerobic exercise is not your thing (if it makes you tired and unable to concentrate), try something less strenuous, like walking. Anxiety interferes with performance, so anything you can do to effectively control and reduce your anxiety will help. Have fun, good luck, and enjoy your lifespan psychology course.

Acknowledgements

Special thanks go to Cornelius Rea, Consulting Psychologist, whose "To the Student" preface for Don and Sandra Hockenbury's *Psychology,* Sixth Edition, served as a guide for crafting this preface. In addition, I would like to thank Eric Dorger, Julio Espin, and Stacey Alexander of Worth Publishers for seeing this book through production.

Lisa Hager
Spring Hill College

Study Guide

Chapter 1

The People and the Field

Welcome to your life. Somewhere in the pages that follow you will get to know yourself and those around you a little more. You will learn why children have a unique perspective on the world, why you and your parents don't always see eye to eye, and why your grandparents prefer to spend time with their grandchildren rather than meeting new people.

You will see what developmental psychologists look for while doing research. You will also see some of the amazingly creative experiments that scientists have developed to gather data. In many cases you will be exposed to data gathered from countries other than the United States. You will see how culture as well as economics and gender influence human development. The basic theories that influence developmentalists are also outlined for you in this chapter.

You will find that ever provocative question "Is it nature or nurture?" throughout the book. In most cases the answer will contain a little of both nature and nurture. We will lean heavily on Piaget's and Erikson's theories to explain behavior, but they will not be the only two theorists we discuss. We will also review the specific structure of research in this field. When you are finished with this book we hope you will be able to recognize data as either correlational or experimental and that you will be able to design your own experimental research using either cross-sectional or longitudinal designs. In this chapter we will discuss the major concepts of developmental psychology, briefly outline the theorists who are discussed throughout the book, and learn how developmentalists use research to answer questions about human development.

Who We Are and What We Study (pages 4–5)

What It's All About

Developmentalists try to understand lifespan development by relying on knowledge from many fields. They try to understand aspects of development that we have in common with one another and the aspects of development that make each of us unique.

What You Need to Know

After you read this section you should be able to:

- Define development and discuss the meaning of lifespan development, including its multidisciplinary structure.

Testing Your Knowledge

The objectives addressed in this section may help you solve problems or understand situations such as that presented in the question below. At the end of this section, with the knowledge you acquire, you should be able to respond to the following question in writing. Answer guides are given at the end of this chapter.

1. Think about your own life experiences and the life experiences of a parent, sibling, or friend. What is one experience that both of you have had? Is this experience one that most people have had? What is one experience that you have had but the other person has not? Is this an experience that most people have? Summarize your responses by using the characteristics of lifespan development.

Setting the Context (pages 5–12)

What It's All About

Look at the people around you. What connects them to one another? Some are older, some are younger. Some are men, some women. Some are from different cultures and speak different languages. They can be rich or poor or living in the middle-income bracket. All of these descriptors are capable of influencing development. In the field of developmental psychology we study the relationship of these variables to the ways we behave and think. In this section we will look at the different contexts within which we develop.

What You Need to Know

After you read this section you should be able to:

- Define the concept of cohort group, and describe how being a part of a particular cohort might impact an individual's life course.
- Describe the biological/social/cultural contexts that influence the life course, such as changing views of life stages, historical events, and socioeconomic status.
- Explain the difference between collectivist and individualistic cultures and their potential impact on cultural values.
- Discuss the impact on development of one or two gender differences.

Testing Your Knowledge

The objectives addressed in this section may help you solve problems or understand situations such as that presented in the question below. At the end of this section, with the knowledge you acquire, you should be able to respond to the following question in writing. Answer guides are given at the end of this chapter.

1. Talk to some family members about your great-grandparents and grandparents. How long did they live? Are they still living? How was their health near the end of their lives? How different will your health be at that age? How much older will you live to be?

Theories: Lenses for Looking at the Lifespan (pages 12–25)

What It's All About

Theories of development explain why people behave or think the way that they do and how behavior and thinking change across the lifespan. Some of the theories you will learn about (e.g., behaviorism) offer broad explanations and attempt to explain many aspects of development while others (e.g., attachment theory) are more specific and attempt to explain certain aspects of development. In your textbook, the theories are organized based on how much they rely on nature or nurture to explain development.

What You Need to Know

After you read this section you should be able to:

- Define the concept of a theory and describe how a theory is useful to those who try to understand development.
- Describe the main idea of behaviorism and discuss how reinforcement operates.
- Discuss the differences between traditional behaviorism and cognitive behaviorism.
- Define self-efficacy and give an example of its potential influence on an individual's functioning.
- Describe the research strategies used in the area of behavioral genetics.
- Compare Bowlby's concept of attachment to the concept of species survival.
- Compare the main ideas of evolutionary psychology and behavioral genetics.
- Define evocative forces and active forces, and discuss the interactive process of nature and nurture.
- Describe Piaget's view of how cognitive growth proceeds.
- Name and describe Piaget's four stages of development.
- Discuss Erik Erikson's eight psychosocial stages of development.
- Describe the developmental systems perspective and the forces that shape development.

Testing Your Knowledge

The objectives addressed in this section may help you solve problems or understand situations such as those presented in the questions below. At the end of this section, with the knowledge you acquire, you should be able to respond to the following questions in writing. Answer guides are given at the end of this chapter.

1. A friend is describing his 4-year-old daughter's preferences for neatness and order. He says his daughter must have inherited these preferences from her mother and asks if you agree or disagree. Use your knowledge of theories of human development to describe how his question is not as simple as he may think.

2. Describe a situation in which you had feelings of self-efficacy.

3. How are Freud's and Bowlby's ideas about attachment similar and different?

4. Apply the developmental systems perspective to your life by identifying specific forces that have shaped you into the person you are today.

Research Methods: The Tools of the Trade (pages 26–32)

What It's All About

Scientific research allows us to test the accuracy of our theories. Researchers in lifespan development rely on the scientific method to guide their approaches to important questions about development. The logic or rationale used to study lifespan development is the same logic or rationale used by biologists, medical researchers, or physicists. There are some methods, however, that are specific to studying human development. These include cross-sectional and longitudinal designs.

What You Need to Know

After you read this section you should be able to:

- Define correlation and experimental research, and discuss their similarities and differences.
- Describe and give examples of cross-sectional and longitudinal studies.
- Critique a research study's sampling and methods.
- Describe the difference between quantitative and qualitative research methods.

Testing Your Knowledge

The objectives addressed in this section may help you solve problems or understand situations such as that presented in the question below. At the end of this section, with the knowledge you acquire, you should be able to respond to the following question in writing. Answer guides are given at the end of this chapter.

1. Your friend is majoring in early childhood education and is working in the afternoons at a local child development center. He has noticed that on some afternoons the children seem to be tired and less able to pay attention than on other afternoons. He thinks this difference may be due to the snacks they get. On some days they get fruit and cheese and on other days they get graham crackers. There are 40 children at the center, and they are divided into two groups for snack. One group gets a snack at 2:00 pm, and the other group gets a snack at 2:15 pm. He wants you to help him test whether the afternoon snack is related to their behavior. He believes that the fruit and cheese snack raises the children's energy and attention levels. What is the best research method for testing his hypothesis? Describe how you would go about setting up the study.

Put It All Together

Matching Items

Match the appropriate term with its definition or description. Answers appear at the end of the chapter.

_____1. people in the same age group

_____2. explanation for why we act the way we do

_____3. looking for what is observable and measurable

_____4. observation without manipulation of variables

_____5. study of all people at a specific point in time

_____6. study of a group of people over many years

_____7. Erik Erikson's theory

_____8. a connection between infant and caregiver

_____9. B. F. Skinner defined this form of conditioning

_____ 10. imitating what you see another person do

_____11. the study of aging

_____12. fitting the world to match our mental structures

_____13. our genetic tendencies produce reactions in others

_____14. people born between 1946 and 1964

_____15. changing our thinking to fit the world

A. cross-sectional
B. longitudinal
C. cohort
D. accommodation
E. naturalistic
F. theory
G. operant
H. modeling
I. evocative forces
J. psychosocial
K. assimilation
L. baby boomers
M. gerontology
N. attachment
O. behaviorism

Multiple-Choice Questions

Circle the best answer for each question. Answers appear at the end of the chapter.

1. Doris is 18-years-old and not sure what her career plan will be. She has thought about going to college, but isn't committed to the idea. What stage of development is Doris experiencing?
   A. adolescence
   B. emerging adulthood
   C. adulthood
   D. young-old

2. Fred is 65, healthy, and active. He is retired, but works part-time teaching business courses at a community college. He spends weekends volunteering at a local food-bank. What stage of development is Fred experiencing?
   A. adulthood
   B. young-old
   C. old-old
   D. pre-geriatric

3. Behaviorists emphasize the role of _____ in development.
   A. nature
   B. nurture
   C. balance
   D. equality

4. According to behaviorists, a response that is NOT reinforced will:
   A. go away (extinguish).
   B. become stronger (amplify).
   C. not become stronger or weaker.
   D. become biologically motivated.

5. According to cognitive behaviorism, individuals:
   A. are biologically preconditioned toward action.
   B. cannot be influenced by others.
   C. learn by watching and imitating what other people do.
   D. gravitate toward the unknown.

6. Piaget's theory says:
   A. a child's understanding of the world is essentially the same as an adult's.
   B. toddlers innately understand the difference between what is real and what is imaginary.
   C. an individual's reaction to new ideas is based on genetic traits.
   D. an individual's assimilation of new ideas leads to accommodation.

7. Andrea designs a questionnaire to measure the level of self-confidence and perceived ability in the mathematical area among tenth graders. What type of measurement strategy is Andrea using?
   A. naturalistic observation
   B. self-reporting
   C. ability testing
   D. observational reporting

8. Andrea incorporates end-of-the-year state testing results in her study. What type of measurement strategy is Andrea using?
   A. naturalistic observation
   B. self-reporting
   C. ability testing
   D. observational reporting

9. Evolutionary psychologists emphasize the role of _____ in development.
   A. nature
   B. nuture
   C. modeling
   D. reinforcement

10. Which of the following would NOT be a probable area of research for a behavioral geneticist?
    A. the identification of genes contributing to substance abuse
    B. the study of identical twins separated in childhood
    C. the study of adopted children and their families
    D. the study of social environment on childhood development

11. Dr. Forest hypothesizes that college students who are distracted in class are less likely to perform well on their exams. She measures how often students text during class and the grades they get on their first exams. This type of research is best described as:
    A. a true experiment.
    B. a longitudinal study.
    C. a self-report strategy.
    D. a correlational study.

12. In order to ensure that the students in her study are similar to most college students, Dr. Forest randomly samples students from several types of classes and from several different colleges. Dr. Forest is making sure that she has:
    A. a representative sample.
    B. qualitative research.
    C. bidirectionality.
    D. a cohort.

13. The lifespan approach to studying development:
    A. studies only young children and older adults.
    B. is only concerned with normal development.
    C. focuses on positive changes in development.
    D. draws on different disciplines.

14. Dr. Black believes that we can best understand development by using multiple approaches and studying how genetics, culture, and socioeconomic status interact. Dr. Black's approach can best be described as a(n):
    A. developmental systems approach.
    B. cognitive-behavioral approach.
    C. evolutionary psychology approach.
    D. behavioral genetics approach.

15. Developmentalists who test groups of people and use numerical scales are doing _____ research, and developmentalists who interview individuals and summarize the content of the interviews are doing _____ research.
    A. cross-sectional; longitudinal
    B. quantitative; qualitative
    C. longitudinal; cross-sectional
    D. qualitative; quantitative

Short-Answer and Essay Questions

Write a few sentences in the space below the question. For longer answers, jot down the points you want to make. Organize your ideas in an outline or other graphic method. Then, write the full essay on a separate piece of paper.

1. Piaget and Erikson both proposed stage theories of development. In a sentence or two summarize each of their theories.

2. Dr. Mose is investigating changes in self-esteem across the lifespan. She brings in five groups of individuals (10-year-olds, 16-year-olds, 25-year-olds, 40-year-olds, and 60-year-olds) and administers a self-esteem scale to each group. She finds that self-esteem is highest in the 40-year-olds and lowest in the 10-year-olds. She concludes that self-esteem increases across the lifespan. What type of design, specific to the study of development, is she using? What are the weaknesses of this design? How could she improve her study and what kind of design should she use?

Answer Key for Chapter 1

Matching Items

1. C	9. G
2. F	10. H
3. O	11. M
4. E	12. K
5. A	13. I
6. B	14. L
7. J	15. D
8. N	

Multiple-Choice Questions

1. B	9. A
2. B	10. D
3. B	11. D
4. A	12. A
5. C	13. D
6. D	14. A
7. B	15. B
8. C	

Short-Answer and Essay Questions

1. **Question:** Piaget and Erikson both propose stage theories of development. In a sentence or two summarize each of their theories.
   Answer guide: Your answer for Piaget should focus on cognitive development, how everyone goes through the same stages in the same order, and how we have a unique perspective on the world during each of the four stages. Your answer for Erikson should focus on personality development, how everyone goes through the same stages in the same order, and during each stage there is a task we must complete before we can successfully move on to the next stage.

2. **Question:** Dr. Mose is investigating changes in self-esteem across the lifespan. She brings in five groups of individuals (10-year-olds, 16-year-olds, 25-year-olds, 40-year-olds, and 60-year-olds) and administers a self-esteem scale to each group. She finds that self-esteem is highest in the 40-year-olds and lowest in the 10-year-olds. She concludes that self-esteem increases across the lifespan. What type of design, specific to the study of development, is she using? What are the weaknesses of this design? How could she improve her study and what kind of design should she use?
   Answer guide: Dr. Mose is using a cross-sectional design. You should describe cohort effects and how they impact cross-sectional studies. A better option would be for her to use a longitudinal design. Explain the advantages of this type of design as compared to the cross-sectional design.

Testing Your Knowledge

Who We Are and What We Study

1. **Question:** Think about your own life experiences and the life experiences of a parent, sibling, or friend. What is one experience that both of you have had? Is this experience one that most people have had? What is one experience that you have had but the other person has not? Is this an experience that most people have? Summarize your responses by using the characteristics of lifespan development.
   Answer guide: You might have used an example like attending college. Using this example you would identify how college attendance is a transition that is often experienced in emerging adulthood (normative) but you may point out that your parent didn't attend college until he/she was in his/her 30s (non-normative) or didn't attend college at all (individual difference between you and your parent). You may also point out that the question of who attends college and when might be of interest to psychologists, educators, and college administrators (multidisciplinary nature of development).

Setting the Context

1. **Question:** Talk to some family members about your great-grandparents and

grandparents. How long did they live? Are they still living? How was their health near the end of their lives? How different will your health be at that age? How much older will you live to be?

Answer guide: Generally speaking you will live longer and can expect to be healthier at an older age than your grandparents and great-grandparents. In your answer did you include factors such as your gender and socioeconomic status? These factors will influence your lifespan.

Theories: Lenses for Looking at the Lifespan

1. **Question:** A friend is describing his 4-year-old daughter's preferences for neatness and order. He says his daughter must have inherited these preferences from her mother and asks if you agree or disagree. Use your knowledge of theories of human development to describe how his question is not as simple as he may think.

   Answer guide: An overriding issue to discuss is the nature versus nurture debate and how evocative forces and bidirectionality play roles in explaining behavior. In your answer you could discuss the roles of reinforcement (behaviorism) and modeling/imitation (cognitive behaviorism), the role of inheritance (behavioral genetics), and the possibility that this is just a stage in his daughter's thinking as she tries to make sense of the world (Piaget). You could also use Erikson's stage of initiative versus guilt to explain how your friend and his daughter's mother should react to the child's behavior. The most important point is that in order to best understand his daughter's behavior we should consider several of these approaches.

2. **Question:** Describe a situation in which you had feelings of self-efficacy.

   Answer guide: There are many possible answers to this question. The main point is that you describe a situation where you felt like you could do something and then you tried to do it. Perhaps you didn't succeed initially but you persisted until you did.

3. **Question:** How are Freud's and Bowlby's ideas about attachment similar and different?

   Answer guide: Both believed that early life experiences are important for forming an attachment response. Bowlby took this a step further by saying that the attachment response is genetic and is important for survival.

4. **Question:** Apply the developmental systems perspective to your own life by identifying specific forces that have shaped you into the person you are today.

   Answer: Your answer should include both micro and macro influences such as attending private school and growing up in a bilingual household.

Research Methods: The Tools of the Trade

1. **Question:** Your friend is majoring in early childhood education and is working in the afternoons at a local child development center. He has noticed that on some afternoons the children seem to be tired and less able to pay attention than on other afternoons. He thinks this difference may be due to the snacks they get. On some days they get fruit and cheese and on other days they get graham crackers. There are 40 children at the center, and they are divided into two groups for snack. One group gets a snack at 2:00 pm, and the other group gets a snack at 2:15 pm. He wants you to help him test whether the afternoon snack is related to their behavior. He believes that the fruit and cheese snack raises the children's energy and attention levels. What is the best research method for testing his hypothesis? Describe how you would go about setting up the study.

   Answer guide: Your friend has already done some observation, but you need something more systematic. You could conduct a correlational study, but this won't tell you whether it is the snack or some other variable that explains your results. A true experiment would be best. You could randomly assign one group to get the fruit and cheese snack and the second group to get the graham cracker snack. This would be your independent variable. Then you could measure how many times the children have to be redirected to the activities they are doing, and/or whether the children are falling asleep during the afternoon (there are other possible measurements you could take). It might also be important to control other variables like day of the week (for example, you may not want to test your hypothesis on Friday when children may be tired or excited about weekend activities) and perhaps to collect data on more than one day and switch the group's snacks so you can see each group's behavior on both types of snacks. Controlling other possible variables is key for experimental research.

Chapter 2

Prenatal Development, Pregnancy, and Birth

While I was still in undergraduate school I took a course in developmental biology. It was in a stadium classroom with more than 200 other students. On the last day of class the professor asked us if there were any comments. I told him it seemed that there were a tremendous number of things that can go wrong and wondered how on earth we make it to birth. His answer was, "Look around the room. It works!"

As a species we don't like to leave things to fate. We want to be able to control our destiny and to do that we rely on many talismans. These can be objects or behaviors that supposedly make the world revolve our way. It is no wonder that superstitious behaviors developed around pregnancy and birth. Both are problematic and, in not-so-ancient times, death was a very possible outcome for baby and mother. Advanced medical interventions have changed that fate, but developing nations don't have advanced medicine, and they still live with fear of the outcome.

As the book states, only 4 percent of pregnancies occur with problems. The problems of pregnancy, however, are not the only fates we want to control. Getting pregnant in the first place can be difficult or nearly impossible. Many societies develop rituals to help women get pregnant and then employ other rituals to keep them healthy when they are expecting. In this chapter we will discuss the issues surrounding getting pregnant, staying healthy during pregnancy, and delivering a healthy child. We will also discuss what can make things go wrong and what happens if there's a problem.

The First Step: Fertilization (pages 38–41)

What It's All About

The first step in a new life is combining the egg (ovum) with the sperm. To understand fertilization you must study some biology. In this section, you will learn about specific structures in the male and female bodies that are important for reproduction. You will also learn about some of the basics of genetics.

What You Need to Know

After you read this section you should be able to:

- Explain the female and male reproductive systems.
- Describe the process of fertilization.
- Explain the role of DNA, including chromosomes and genes, in fertilization.

Testing Your Knowledge

The objectives addressed in this section may help you solve problems or understand situations such as that presented in the question below. At the end of this section, with the knowledge you acquire, you should be able to respond to the following question in writing. Answer guides are given at the end of this chapter.

1. Describe the process of fertilization beginning with ovulation and ending with the sperm penetrating the egg.

Prenatal Development (pages 41–45)

What It's All About

Most of the changes that occur in making an adult human happen from fertilization to birth. There are more changes occurring during prenatal development than at any other time, so this is the time when most of the problems arise. However, there are more than six billion people on the Earth, so the process works. This period of human life can be broken into three stages which are distinguished by the position and amount of development of the cells. We can also arbitrarily break the gestation time into three evenly divided trimesters. In this section, we will discuss the three stages of development. We will also briefly look at the overall pattern of human development.

What You Need to Know

After you read this section you should be able to:

- Describe the development of the zygote and blastocyst in the process of implantation, which begins the germinal stage of prenatal development.
- Describe the development of the neural tube and other major body structures as part of the embryonic stage of prenatal development.
- Identify principles of prenatal development as the proximodistal sequence (inner to outer), the cephalocaudal sequence (top to bottom), and the mass-to-specific sequence (large to small).
- Describe prenatal development during the fetal stage, including the age of viability—the earliest point at which the baby can survive outside of the womb.

Testing Your Knowledge

The objectives addressed in this section may help you solve problems or understand situations such as those presented in the questions below. At the end of this section, with the knowledge you acquire, you should be able to respond to the following questions in writing. Answer guides are given at the end of this chapter.

1. A friend is 8 weeks pregnant. Describe for her the systems that have developed and the growth that has occurred in her embryo.

2. Think about prenatal development and give an example of the proximodistal sequence, the cephalocaudal sequence, and the mass-to-specific sequence.

Pregnancy (pages 45–49)

What It's All About

This section is all about the way the woman feels from pregnancy to birth and the role of the expectant father. As the chapter says, the way a woman feels will be dependent on many factors, including her economic situation, social support, and overall health. In this section, we will talk about those things.

What You Need to Know

After you read this section you should be able to:

- Identify and describe symptoms and experiences of the first, second, and third trimesters of pregnancy for both the mother and father, as well as for mothers without optimal circumstances or support.

Testing Your Knowledge

The objectives addressed in this section may help you solve problems or understand situations such as that presented in the question below. At the end of this section, with the knowledge you acquire, you should be able to respond to the following question in writing. Answer guides are given at the end of this chapter.

1. Your friend just got pregnant and is wondering what to expect. What can you tell her?

Threats to the Developing Baby (pages 49–62)

What It's All About

Most babies are born healthy, but a minority (about 4 percent) do have some type of birth defect. Birth defects may be due to teratogens, which are substances that can cross the placental barrier and harm the unborn baby. HIV infection and alcohol are both examples of teratogens. Birth defects may also be due to genetic abnormalities. Genetic abnormalities refer to instances where the unborn baby receives too many, too few, or damaged copies of chromosomes. In this section you will learn about some of the most common teratogens and chromosomal disorders, you will learn more about genetics, you will be introduced to procedures that can be used for the early detection of teratogenic effects and genetic abnormalities, and you will learn about assisted reproductive technology (ART).

What You Need to Know

After you read this section you should be able to:

- Identify teratogens as substances that cross the placenta and harm the fetus.
- Identify chromosomal and genetic disorders that threaten the fetus, including Down syndrome and single-gene disorders, dominant disorders, recessive disorders, and sex-linked single-gene disorders.
- Describe genetic counseling and genetic testing available to pregnant women and couples.
- Describe prenatal tests, including ultrasound, chorionic villus sampling, and amniocentesis.
- Explain infertility and interventions such as assisted reproductive technology (ART) and in vitro fertilization.

Testing Your Knowledge

The objectives addressed in this section may help you solve problems or understand situations such as that presented in the question below. At the end of this section, with the knowledge you acquire, you should be able to respond to the following question in writing. Answer guides are given at the end of this chapter.

1. Someone you know is worried about the genetic problems that can occur with their unborn child. You are not a genetic counselor, but you can give that person some of the answers now that you have read this section.

2. A couple you know has tried to get pregnant for more than six months. What can you tell them?

Birth (pages 62–66)

What It's All About

Birth in the United States, for mother and child, is much safer than it used to be. There are parts of the world, however, where birth is still dangerous. In this section, you will learn about the stages of birth and birth options of the past and the present.

What You Need to Know

After you read this section you should be able to:

- Describe each of the three stages of birth: dilation and effacement (stage 1), birth (stage 2), the expulsion of the placenta (stage 3).
- Identify threats that may occur during birth and birth options from the past and present, including natural birth and cesarean section.

Testing Your Knowledge

The objectives addressed in this section may help you solve problems or understand situations such as that presented in the question below. At the end of this section, with the knowledge you acquire, you should be able to respond to the following question in writing. Answer guides are given at the end of this chapter.

1. A woman you know is unsure about giving birth in a hospital. She wants other options, but everyone she knows was born in a hospital. Explain her options and their accompanying costs and benefits.

The Newborn (pages 66–70)

What It's All About

Once a baby is born it is weighed and several behavioral and physiological functions are evaluated. Babies with low birth weight have an increased risk of future health problems and are more likely to die within the first year of life. In this section you will learn about newborn assessment, infant mortality, and the impact of socioeconomic status on low birth weight and infant mortality.

What You Need to Know

After you read this section you should be able to:

- Explain the Apgar scale, a quick test that monitors the baby's condition.
- Identify threats to the development of the neonate from being of low birth weight or very low birth weight.
- Describe infant mortality rates and the link between infant mortality and socioeconomic status.
- Point out the bonding of baby to parent, which occurs in a variety of forms of families.

Testing Your Knowledge

The objectives addressed in this section may help you solve problems or understand situations such as that presented in the question below. At the end of this section, with the knowledge you acquire, you should be able to respond to the following question in writing. Answer guides are given at the end of this chapter.

1. Your friend's relatives are in the waiting room and have just been told the sex and weight of the baby to which she just gave birth. The relatives are nervous about the newborn's health. What can you tell them?

Put It All Together

Matching Items

Match the appropriate term with its definition or description. Answers appear at the end of the chapter.

_____ 1. growth from top to bottom
_____ 2. growth from the inside out
_____ 3. normally 267 days from conception to birth
_____ 4. when the baby starts kicking in the womb
_____ 5. a substance that affects neonatal development
_____ 6. when a single gene is needed for expression
_____ 7. when both genes are needed for expression
_____ 8. when the gene is on the X or Y chromosome
_____ 9. using a noninvasive procedure to see the fetus
_____ 10. using a needle to get fluid to test the fetus's genetics
_____ 11. houses the developing baby
_____ 12. houses the eggs
_____ 13. provides nutrients for the developing baby
_____ 14. cluster of cells before implantation
_____ 15. where sperm are manufactured

A. uterus
B. amniocentesis
C. recessive
D. ovary
E. quickening
F. dominant
G. placenta
H. proximodistal
I. ultrasound
J. testes
K. cephalocaudal
L. gestation
M. blastocyst
N. sex-linked
O. teratogen

Multiple-Choice Questions

Circle the best answer for each question. Answers appear at the end of the chapter.

1. Prior to cell division, the fertilized ovum is referred to as a(n):
    A. egg.
    B. zygote.
    C. embryo.
    D. fetus.

2. The first nine days after fertilization when the cell mass has NOT yet attached to the uterus is referred to as the _____ stage.
    A. ovulation
    B. germinal
    C. embryonic
    D. fetal

3. The period from the third week to the eighth week of pregnancy during which major organs are formed is referred to as the _____ stage.
   A. ovulation
   B. germinal
   C. embryonic
   D. fetal

4. The period from the ninth week of pregnancy to birth is referred to as the _____ stage.
   A. ovulation
   B. germinal
   C. embryonic
   D. fetal

5. C-sections account for what percentage of births in the United States?
   A. 1 percent
   B. 33 percent
   C. 57 percent
   D. 73 percent

6. Fetal alcohol syndrome (FAS) may be characterized by:
   A. facial deformities and impaired physical development.
   B. emotional and developmental disabilities.
   C. hyperactivity and memory deficits.
   D. All of the above.

7. Down syndrome is caused by:
   A. an extra chromosome in pair number 21.
   B. an extra Y chromosome.
   C. a virus present in the uterus.
   D. excessive alcohol.

8. At what week does the baby have at least a 50/50 chance of survival?
   A. 22
   B. 23
   C. 25
   D. 28

9. The germinal, embryonic, and fetal stages refer to the pregnancy from _____ perspective while the first, second, and third trimesters refer to the pregnancy from _____ perspective.
   A. the unborn baby's; the mother's
   B. the scientific; the unscientific
   C. the mother's; the unborn baby's
   D. the unscientific; the scientific

10. DNA consists of:
    A. chromosomes.
    B. trisomy 21.
    C. genes.
    D. hormones.

11. Newborns with 5-minute Apgar scale scores above ____ are considered to be in excellent condition.
    A. 2
    B. 5
    C. 7
    D. 9

12. Compared to other affluent countries, the infant mortality rate in the United States is:
    A. about the same as those countries.
    B. significantly worse than those countries.
    C. significantly better than those countries.
    D. difficult to assess due to incomplete data.

13. The mass-to-specific sequence of development means that the embryo's:
    A. eyes will develop before its head.
    B. fingers will develop before its hands.
    C. legs will develop before its torso.
    D. feet will develop before its toes.

14. Which of the following is not a natural childbirth option?
    A. getting a cesarean section
    B. getting a doula
    C. using the Lamaze method
    D. using the Bradley method

Short-Answer and Essay Questions

Write a few sentences in the space below the question. For longer answers, jot down the points you want to make. Organize your ideas in an outline or other graphic method. Then, write the full essay on a separate piece of paper.

1. What factors may influence whether a pregnancy is a positive or negative experience?
   (Note: This question is not about the outcome of the pregnancy but is about the actual pregnancy.)

2. For each of the following threats to the developing baby, list whether the threat is: (a) due to a teratogen, a chromosomal problem, or a genetic disorder; (b) how the threat is transmitted to the unborn baby; (c) whether the threat is preventable and how; and (d) what kinds of complications does the threat lead to?

   a.　　　FAS

   b.　　　Down syndrome

   c.　　　Rubella

d.   Tay-Sachs disease

e.   Hemophilia

Answer Key for Chapter 2

Matching Items

1.	K	9.	I
2.	H	10.	B
3.	L	11.	A
4.	E	12.	D
5.	O	13.	G
6.	F	14.	M
7.	C	15.	J
8.	N		

Multiple-Choice Questions

1.	B	8.	C
2.	B	9.	A
3.	C	10.	C
4.	D	11.	C
5.	B	12.	B
6.	D	13.	D
7.	A	14.	A

Short-Answer and Essay Questions

1. **Question:** What factors may influence whether a pregnancy is a positive or negative experience? (Note: This question is not about the outcome of the pregnancy but is about the actual pregnancy.)

   Answer guide: You could simply make a list (health, SES, stress, social supports at home, a doctor's care, social services), but it's always more helpful to give options in complete sentences. Here is that same list in an essay form:

   Many factors under human control can improve the experience of pregnancy. A mother's health is a factor. The healthier the mother is, the higher the possibility of a positive experience. SES, especially on the low end and combined with stress, can lessen the experience. High levels of positive family support improve the mother's feelings about the pregnancy. Doctor's care and social services are types of support required for good physical and mental health.

2. **Question:** For each of the following threats to the developing baby, list whether the threat is: (a) due to a teratogen, a chromosomal problem, or a genetic disorder; (b) how the threat is transmitted to the unborn baby; (c) whether the threat is preventable and how; and (d) what kinds of complications does the threat lead to?

   a. FAS

   b. Down syndrome

   c. Rubella

   d. Tay-Sachs disease

   e. Hemophilia

   Answer guide:

   a. FAS is due to a teratogen and is 100 percent preventable. Don't forget to describe the cognitive, behavioral, and physical effects that can result.

   b. Down syndrome is due to a chromosomal problem. Explain what the chromosomal problem is, and that Down syndrome is not preventable. Don't forget to describe early detection and the cognitive and physical effects that can accompany Down syndrome.

   c. Rubella results from a teratogen; describe how it can be prevented. Be sure to explain that Rubella is only a problem if contracted during a particular stage of development. Don't forget to describe the cognitive and physical effects that can result.

   d. Tay-Sachs disease is a genetic disorder that is located on a recessive gene. Explain this process and how the disease is not preventable but can be detected before the baby is born. Don't forget to describe cognitive and physical effects that can result, and to discuss genetic testing.

e. Hemophilia is a sex-linked genetic disorder. Explain this process, the symptoms of the disorder, and its treatment.

Testing Your Knowledge

The First Step: Fertilization

1. **Question:** Describe the process of fertilization beginning with ovulation and ending with the sperm penetrating the egg.
Answer guide: You should begin your answer with the release of the mature ovum from the ovary. Don't forget to describe the roles of hormones, the fallopian tubes, and sperm.

Prenatal Development

1. **Question:** A friend is eight weeks pregnant. Describe for her the systems that have developed and the growth that has occurred in her embryo.
Answer guide: You should describe the development of the circulatory system and the heartbeat as well as the beginnings of the nervous system including the neural tube. By the eighth week the internal organs are in place and the embryo has arms, legs, fingers, toes, and eyes. It is about the length of a thumb.

2. **Question:** Think about prenatal development and give an example of the proximodistal sequence, the cephalocaudal sequence, and the mass-to-specific sequence.
Answer guide: There are several possible answers to this question. For an example of the proximodistal sequence, describe development that begins in the center of the body and moves outward. You could describe the development of the torso before arms and legs. For an example of cephalocaudal sequence, describe the development that begins at the top of the unborn baby. You could describe the development of the brain and head occurring before development of the legs. For an example of mass-to-specific sequence, describe large structures developing before refinements. You could describe the development of the brain before the eyes.

Pregnancy

1. **Question:** Your friend just got pregnant and is wondering what to expect. What can you tell her?
Answer guide: Each person is different but some of the reports are: Some women feel better than ever before; strong social support is highly important; morning sickness protects the baby (small nibbles all day are better than full meals); some research suggests morning sickness helps bring the child to term; crackers and bread products help with morning sickness; 33 percent of women never get morning sickness. How old is this person? Her age will change the possibility of miscarriage. Quickening at 18 weeks will finally connect the mother to the child.

Threats to the Developing Baby

1. **Question:** Someone you know is worried about the genetic problems that can occur with their unborn child. You are not a genetic counselor, but you can give that person some of the answers now that you have read this section.
Answer guide: How old are the couple? In their 20s they do not have much chance of Down syndrome. Huntington and Tay-Sachs are inherited, so is there any of either in the family history? Tests can determine the presence of those genetic diseases. Did you consider if the couple is black? This increases the chance of sickle cell. Most of the diseases that killed in the past are treatable today. Did you remember which are not?

2. **Question:** A couple you know has tried to get pregnant for more than six months. What can you tell them?
Answer guide: How old are they? If they are under 30, they have not tried long enough. Suggest they keep trying! Lots of options exist including adoption and foster care. If they really want one of their own, they can try a few medical techniques you can name. Remember you have to tell them the probability of success and how much these interventions cost!

Birth

1. **Question:** A woman you know is unsure about giving birth in a hospital. She wants other options, but everyone she knows was

born in a hospital. Explain her options, and their accompanying costs and benefits.

Answer guide: If she wants a c-section she must be in a hospital—a c-section is surgery. Otherwise, she has many options you can now name.

The Newborn

1. **Question:** Your friend's relatives are in the waiting room and have just been told the sex and weight of the baby to which she just gave birth. The relatives are nervous about the newborn's health. What can you tell them?

Answer guide: Do not assume the weight given was normal. Give examples of what you would say at different weights. What is normal weight? You can give them the probability of health based on weight. LBW could be problematic. VLBW is certainly problematic. Include the issues surrounding VLBW. Did you include the costs of VLBW children? Did you consider the SES of the couple or assume they were at your level? How would a different SES change what you said? We know that girls are hardier. Did you take into consideration the sex of the child in your answer?

Chapter 3

Infancy: Physical and Cognitive Development

For just a moment, close your eyes and imagine a newborn baby. Did you picture a bubbly, cuddly, 8-pound bundle of joy?

In the United States we seldom experience the ravaging environmental problems that exist in the developing world. We also have a higher standard of health care, but that, ironically, may cause problems. Our health care system can save many premature and low birth weight infants from death, but those infants often have health problems that other countries don't experience. One problem that exists throughout the world, however, is sudden infant death syndrome.

The meaning of the word infant is "without speech." Infants can't tell us what is happening to them, what they think, or what they see or hear. Even though they can't tell us about themselves, some remarkable experiments give us a basic understanding of the life of the infant. In this chapter we will see how the baby develops in its early life outside the womb. We will also look at the normal developmental processes of body and brain growth, sleeping, eating, crying, and sensory, motor, cognitive, and language development. We will explore some cultural and individual differences.

Setting the Context (pages 78–80)

What It's All About

At birth, the brain has more neurons than it needs but is still only 25 percent of its adult weight. What happens to those extra neurons and how does the brain lose neurons but gain weight? In this section you will learn about the basic structures of neurons and the important concepts of neural pruning and brain plasticity.

What You Need to Know

After you read this section you should be able to:

- Explain the physical growth and development of the infant brain, especially the cerebral cortex, brain volume, and neurons.
- Understand the processes of synaptogenesis and myelination.
- Point out the need for neural pruning.
- Explain the phenomenon of brain plasticity.

Testing Your Knowledge

The objectives addressed in this section may help you solve problems or understand situations such as that presented in the question below. At the end of this section, with the knowledge you acquire, you should be able to respond to the following question in writing. Answer guides are given at the end of this chapter.

1. Our brains grow and we lose neurons. Explain this apparent contradiction.

Basic Newborn States (pages 80–92)

What It's All About

Have you ever met a newborn baby? They spend most of their time sleeping. When they aren't sleeping they are often crying or eating. In this section you will learn about the three main activities for newborns—eating, crying, and sleeping.

What You Need to Know

After you read this section you should be able to:
- Discuss the automatic reflexes of sucking and rooting in newborns.
- Understand the significance of 2-year-old food caution.
- Understand the inherent benefits and the physical deterrents associated with breastfeeding.
- Describe the devastating effects of malnutrition and undernutrition in infants and children.
- List and describe the three main federal programs designed to feed infants (Food Stamp Program; Special Supplemental Nutrition Program for Women, Infants, and Children; and Child and Adult Care Food Program).
- Explain the important role of crying in infants' expression of needs.
- Learn techniques to quiet a crying baby (swaddling, pacifiers, skin-to-skin contact, kangaroo care, massage, and so on).
- Describe a newborn's pattern of consciousness and sleep.
- Explore ways to help babies learn to self-soothe.
- Present the pros and cons of co-sleeping.
- Point out the unpredictable incidences of Sudden Infant Death Syndrome (SIDS) and the importance of the Back to Sleep program.

Testing Your Knowledge

The objectives addressed in this section may help you solve problems or understand situations such as those presented in the questions below. At the end of this section, with the knowledge you acquire, you should be able to respond to the following questions in writing. Answer guides are given at the end of this chapter.

1. A friend has just had a baby and has come to you for support in her decision to bottle feed. What would you tell her?

2. A friend has a 1-month-old son who cries continuously, and she is worried about the child. What can you tell your friend to help calm her concerns?

3. A friend has a 2-month-old daughter who only sleeps for an hour before waking up. This friend picks the child up as soon as he sees it is awake. He does this to keep the child from feeling abandoned. What would you tell him about his behavior?

Sensory and Motor Development (pages 92–98)

What It's All About

Infants are born legally blind, but they can see. What do they see? Do they have preferences? Infants obviously can't throw a baseball. But even when they develop the skill to throw something, the intricacies of a curve ball take even more time to develop. A baby's growth occurs in specific patterns. Babies grow from top to bottom, and outward from the sides. They also develop very coarse movements before they develop finesse. Walking comes after crawling, which follows the not-so-simple act of turning over. This section discusses the infant's developing motor skills and sensations.

What You Need to Know

After you read this section you should be able to:

- Discuss the functioning level of each of an infant's five senses immediately after birth up through the first birthday (hearing, smell, taste, touch, and sight).
- Describe the preferential-looking paradigm, habituation, and face perception studies.
- Describe the infant's development of depth perception and the research significance of the visual cliff.
- Explain infant motor development and corresponding milestones.
- Understand the importance of baby-proofing a home.

Testing Your Knowledge

The objectives addressed in this section may help you solve problems or understand situations such as those presented in the questions below. At the end of this section, with the knowledge you acquire, you should be able to respond to the following questions in writing. Answer guides are given at the end of this chapter.

1. Your friend is leaving her newborn at her aunt's house so that she can return to work. She is thinking about leaving a picture of herself in a frame on the crib so her infant will be able to see her during the day. You tell her this is a great idea. Now explain what she should consider when choosing a picture.

2. Your child just started crawling. What safety issues do you need to be aware of?

Cognition (pages 98–104)

What It's All About

Infants are constantly exploring their worlds through watching, touching, and putting objects in their mouths. Jean Piaget was one of the first individuals to systematically study the cognitive skills of infants and children. Piaget believed that infants have their own special way of understanding the world and that cognitive development begins with the sucking reflex and ends with language. In this section, you will learn about Piaget's sensorimotor stage of cognitive development and how Piaget wasn't always correct in his assumptions about what infants can and cannot do. You will also see how early cognitive abilities play a role in how we relate to others.

What You Need to Know

After you read this section you should be able to:

- Describe Piaget's stage of cognitive development associated with infancy (sensorimotor stage, primary circular reactions, secondary circular reactions, and tertiary circular reactions).
- Present criticisms of Piaget's theory.
- Describe some indicators of social cognition, such as joint attention, in infants.

Testing Your Knowledge

The objectives addressed in this section may help you solve problems or understand situations such as those presented in the questions below. At the end of this section, with the knowledge you acquire, you should be able to respond to the following questions in writing. Answer guides are given at the end of this chapter.

1. You watch as a friend hides a baby's toy and tries to play hide and seek with the child. The baby has no interest in the toy once it is out of sight. Tell your friend why and give another example of the same phenomenon.

2. Your roommate believes that everyone in the field of psychology accepts Piaget's theory of infant cognitive development as "the truth." Explain to him why his belief is incorrect.

Language: The Endpoint of Infancy (pages 105–107)

What It's All About

Human language is quite remarkable. We have the ability of stringing together an infinite number of word combinations. Many scientists believe that human beings are born with the capability of producing language and as social beings we are motivated to communicate with others. Babies all over the world go through the same stages of language development at about the same time. Language begins with cooing sounds that develop into babbling then the use of one word and finally the ability to string together many words. In this section, you will learn about historical and current views of language development, the stages of language development, and how adults use a special type of speech with babies.

What You Need to Know

After you read this section you should be able to:

- Describe historial and current views of language development.
- Explain the roots and milestones of speech/language in infants.

Testing Your Knowledge

The objectives addressed in this section may help you solve problems or understand situations such as that presented in the question below. At the end of this section, with the knowledge you acquire, you should be able to respond to the following question in writing. Answer guides are given at the end of this chapter.

1. In our childhood my sister and I used to race to finish our bowls of cereal. Her first real sentence was "I beat," exuberantly exclaimed upon her first victory. About how old do you think she was, and what stages of speech had she entered and passed through?

Put It All Together

Matching Items

Match the appropriate term with its definition or description. Answers appear at the end of the chapter.

_____ 1. long extension of the neuron
_____ 2. neuronal structure for incoming signals
_____ 3. the space between two neurons
_____ 4. condition due to malnutrition
_____ 5. bad stomach cramps in babies
_____ 6. back to sleep program reduces this problem
_____ 7. the hypothetical structure that helps us learn language
_____ 8. simplified, exaggerated, high-pitched speech
_____ 9. when a child puts itself back to sleep
_____ 10. using a sling to carry the infant
_____ 11. when a baby becomes bored with looking at an object
_____ 12. performing a different action to get to a goal
_____ 13. idea that babies are passionate to communicate
_____ 14. vocal circular reactions
_____ 15. touch on the cheek stimulates baby to turn his/her head

A. colic
B. kangaroo care
C. LAD
D. social-interactionist view
E. axon
F. babbling
G. self-soothing
H. synapse
I. rooting reflex
J. means-end behavior
K. IDS
L. stunting
M. habituation
N. SIDS
O. dendrite

Multiple-Choice Questions

Circle the best answer for each question. Answers appear at the end of the chapter.

1. The _____ is the site of every conscious perception, action, and thought.
   A. synapses
   B. cerebral cortex
   C. axons
   D. dendrites

2. What is the brain's process of developing interconnections with other neurons called?
   A. synaptogenesis
   B. myelination
   C. axon resilience
   D. fetal cortex development

3. Which of the following is NOT a newborn reflex?
   A. sucking in reaction to stimulation on the cheek
   B. grasping objects that touch the hand
   C. swimming motions if placed underwater
   D. eating only familiar foods

4. Which of the following is true about breast-feeding?
   A. Breast milk provides immunities to middle ear infections and gastrointestinal problems.
   B. Breast-fed babies are more alert during their first weeks after birth.
   C. Breast-fed babies tend to perform better on intelligence tests.
   D. All of the above.

5. About _____ U.S. households with children is/are food insecure.
   A. 1 in 3
   B. 1 in 5
   C. 1 in 10
   D. 3 in 10

6. Recent research indicates that SIDS is linked to an abnormality in the:
   A. cerebral cortex.
   B. frontal lobes.
   C. genes.
   D. brainstem.

7. According to Piaget's theories, the first 2 years of life are spent exploring the world and developing an understanding of how the world works. What is this stage called?
   A. sensorimotor
   B. preoperations
   C. concrete operations
   D. formal operations

8. Piaget believed the sensorimotor stage was divided into three action-oriented stages during which the infant is capable of acquiring new levels of understanding. What are the repetitive actions within these stages sometimes termed?
   A. circular reactions
   B. preoperational instincts
   C. cognitive levels
   D. little scientist reactions

9. Today, it is believed that:
   A. infants grasp the basics of physical reality at a younger age than Piaget believed.
   B. infants' understanding of physical reality emerges very quickly during the first six months.
   C. Piaget overestimated the capability of infants.
   D. infants cannot tell fantasy from reality until they are 1-month-old.

10. Parents can expect first words to occur at:
    A. 1 to 6 months of age.
    B. 10 to 12 months of age.
    C. 12 to 24 months.
    D. after year 2.

11. Extremely simple sentences consisting of bare essentials ("Me up.") are examples of:
    A. cooing.
    B. babbling.
    C. holophrases.
    D. telegraphic speech.

12. Based on face perception studies with infants, which of the following do infants NOT prefer?
    A. faces that are looking directly at them
    B. pictures of their mother's face versus strangers' faces
    C. attractive faces versus unattractive faces
    D. cartoon faces versus photographs

13. By _____ months of age, babies can only discriminate faces from their own ethnic group.
    A. 3
    B. 6
    C. 9
    D. 12

14. When 4-month-old Gabby's father hides her favorite toy under a pillow, Gabby does not try to search for it. Gabby has not yet developed:
    A. object permanence.
    B. habituation.
    C. joint attention.
    D. social cognition.

15. According to Piaget, babies in this stage get into everything.
    A. symbolic thought
    B. little scientist
    C. means-end behavior
    D. reflexive

16. Because of this characteristic, our brains can redirect neurons to serve other functions if we have a brain injury in infancy or childhood.
    A. synaptogenesis
    B. myelination
    C. plasticity
    D. stunting

17. In this stage of sensorimotor development, an infant's habits center on the environment.
    A. primary circular reactions
    B. secondary circular reactions
    C. tertiary circular reactions
    D. semi-circular reactions

18. In this stage of sensorimotor development, an infant's habits center on his/her body.
    A. primary circular reactions
    B. secondary circular reactions
    C. tertiary circular reactions
    D. semi-circular reactions

Short-Answer and Essay Question

Write a few sentences in the space below the question. For longer answers, jot down the points you want to make. Organize your ideas in an outline or other graphic method. Then, write the full essay on a separate piece of paper.

1. Parents love to give advice to their adult children when their children become parents. Your mother is no different. Your older sister just had a baby and your mom tells her to never, ever pick up the baby when he cries because he is just crying for attention, she should never let the baby sleep with her, and she should never use baby talk with the baby. Fortunately, you are taking a developmental psychology class and share your newly acquired knowledge with your sister. What would you tell your sister about these three pieces of advice given by your mother?

Answer Key for Chapter 3

Matching Items

1. E		9. G	
2. O		10. B	
3. H		11. M	
4. L		12. J	
5. A		13. D	
6. N		14. F	
7. C		15. I	
8. K			

Multiple-Choice Questions

1. B		10. B	
2. A		11. D	
3. D		12. D	
4. D		13. C	
5. B		14. A	
6. D		15. B	
7. A		16. C	
8. A		17. B	
9. A		18. A	

Short-Answer and Essay Question

1. **Question:** Parents love to give advice to their adult children when their children become parents. Your mother is no different. Your older sister just had a baby and your mom tells her to never, ever pick up the baby when he cries because he is just crying for attention, she should never let the baby sleep with her, and she should never use baby talk with the baby. Fortunately, you are taking a developmental psychology class and share your newly acquired knowledge with your sister. What would you tell your sister about these three pieces of advice given by your mother?
   Answer guide: Crying—You need to tell your sister that it depends on how old the baby is. For the first 2 months, she should respond to the baby's cries. You may want to describe some of the things that help to soothe a baby. If a baby has been fed, is dry, and there's no reason to suspect the baby is in pain, after 2 months she may want to let the baby cry so he can learn to self-soothe. She may want to ask her doctor about possible colic. Co-sleeping—describe the stereotypes and evidence against them. Caution her that the baby could smother if he is sleeping on his stomach so she would need to be careful. Baby talk—tell her that psychologists call this infant-directed speech (IDS) and describe some of the research that says IDS is helpful for infants.

Testing Your Knowledge

Setting the Context

1. **Question:** Our brains grow and we lose neurons. Explain this apparent contradiction.
   Answer guide: Your answer should describe synaptogenesis, myelination, and pruning.

Basic Newborn States

1. **Question:** A friend has just had a baby and has come to you for support in her decision to bottle-feed. What would you tell her?
   Answer guide: What about her health? Is she AIDS positive? Did you mention the immunity-conferring properties of breast milk? Her job is an important consideration. A breast pump can be used to express the milk and a bottle can be used to feed it to the child while she is at work. What do all the health agencies say about breast-feeding?

2. **Question:** A friend has a 1-month-old son who cries continuously and she is worried about the child. What can you tell your friend to help calm her concerns?
   Answer guide: Did you include information about colic in your answer? At what age does colic stop? How long should she expect colic to continue? Did you consider that the child might be temperamental? What about a person-environment fit for a temperamental

baby? Did you include the methods researchers have studied to quiet infants?

3. **Question:** A friend has a 2-month-old daughter who only sleeps for an hour before waking up. This friend picks the child up as soon as he sees it is awake. He does this to keep the child from feeling abandoned. What would you tell him about his behavior?

   Answer guide: Self-soothing is an important goal. Did you include information in your answer about how his behavior will affect self-soothing? Did you also include the information about the reflexive age of infants and that learning to self-soothe occurs after the age of 12 months. Did you mention the controversy on this issue that exists within psychology?

Sensory and Motor Development

1. **Question:** Your friend is leaving her newborn at her aunt's house so that she can return to work. She is thinking about leaving a picture of herself in a frame on the crib so her infant will be able to see her during the day. You tell her this is a great idea. Now explain what she should consider when choosing a picture.

   Answer guide: Your answer should describe the research on face perception in infants. Infants prefer faces so it should be a head shot because they can differentiate between their mother's face and the faces of strangers. She should be looking directly at the camera, and she may want to consider substituting new pictures after a few weeks with one picture since infants habituate.

2. **Question:** Your child just started crawling. What safety issues do you need to be aware of?

   Answer guide: Did you include items such as stairs, heating grates on the floors, dog and cat food, litter boxes, sharp objects, items that can be pulled off of tables or desks by tablecloths or covers, water dishes, curtains, and electrical outlets? Take the perspective of the child. Get down on all fours and look at our world with an eye for exploration. Think without boundaries, because your child has none.

Cognition

1. **Question:** You watch as a friend hides a baby's toy and tries to play hide-and-seek with the child. The baby has no interest in the toy once it is out of sight. Tell your friend why and give another example of the same phenomenon.

   Answer guide: This is an example of a child who has not reached the stage of object permanence. Did you estimate the age of the child in your answer? At what age will your friend be able to play this game? Did you include an explanation of object permanence in your answer? Did you discuss the psychologist who first studied this stage of life and what he called it? What other problems can be caused by a child in the stage that includes object permanence?

Language: The Endpoint of Infancy

1. **Question:** In our childhood my sister and I used to race to finish our bowls of cereal. Her first real sentence was "I beat," exuberantly exclaimed upon her first victory. About how old do you think she was and what stages of speech had she entered and passed through?

   Answer guide: She was about 18 to 24 months old, the age at which children enter the telegraphic stage of speech. She babbled and used holophrases before entering the telegraphic stage. During this new stage of speech she is expected to gain vocabulary rapidly. Most sentences will show an understanding of grammar, but they will only be made up of two words, like "I beat!" and not "Beat I!"

Chapter 4

Infancy: Socioemotional Development

How does an infant grow into a fully functioning person? What are the social and emotional challenges to growing up? Genetics certainly play a role. No child is like another. Some are shy, some bold, some exuberant, and some depressed. Environment also has its role. We do not live in isolation. We need to socialize and bond with someone. To get a good start, an attachment to one's caregiver is important. Insecure attachments mean trouble in the short term. The good (and bad) news is that attachment is not stable. An insecurely attached child can become securely attached (and vice versa).

Attachment isn't everything. An infant needs the right nutrition, as we saw in the last chapter. He/she needs an environment that fosters trust and the ability to venture out on one's own. Hopefully, every child will live in an environment that fits his/her temperament, with parents that are able to connect with the child. Although we are a wealthy nation, poverty still plays a role in millions of U.S. children's lives. With families relying on more than two incomes, children are regularly placed in daycare services. The quality of that child care is also an issue in development. In this chapter we will visit the issues of attachment, poverty, child care, and the development of autonomy.

Attachment: The Basic Life Bond (pages 112–122)

What It's All About

Babies of many species, including humans, get attached to their caregivers. This attachment is necessary for proper social and emotional development. In this section we will discuss the major impact of attachment.

What You Need to Know

After you read this section you should be able to:

- Define attachment and discuss its importance as a basic human need.
- Explain the historical development of the attachment concept during the twentieth century, especially in relationship to the work of John Bowlby, Konrad Lorenz, and Harry Harlow.
- Describe the various attachment stages: preattachment, attachment in the making, and clear-cut attachment.
- Point out attachment responses in infants, from the social smile to separation or stranger anxiety and social referencing.
- Describe the Strange Situation and the various attachment styles such as secure, insecure, avoidant, anxious-ambivalent, and disorganized.

- Explore the attachment dance between caregiver and baby, especially the effect of temperament that helps produce either synchrony or forms of distress.
- Explore the universality of attachment.
- Describe how early attachment predicts later development.
- Describe the results of research conducted with institutionalized infants and toddlers in Romania.

Testing Your Knowledge

The objectives addressed in this section may help you solve problems or understand situations such as that presented in the question below. At the end of this section, with the knowledge you acquire, you should be able to respond to the following question in writing. Answer guides are given at the end of this chapter.

1. Your friend has a 3-week-old baby and says she feels like all she does is feed the baby, change her diapers, respond to her cries, and do laundry. She also does all of this in a fog because of her sleep deprivation. She wonders if her baby even knows or cares who is doing these things for her. In order to reassure your friend, you want to describe the attachment response and the ensuing dance between child and caregiver. What kinds of things will you tell her?

Settings for Development (pages 122–129)

What It's All About

There is debate over what constitutes poverty in the United States. If we use the current political definition, over 25 percent of children in the United States live in poverty. If we use the social welfare definition of poverty, we can increase that to 44 percent. With all the problems that poverty brings it is no wonder we have so many problems in our society. Single parents are hardest hit; and to stay ahead of the poverty line, many two-parent families are now three-income households. When both parents work, the children often go to day care. There is little time for the parent to interact with the child. In this section, we will discuss the impact of poverty and child care on the social and emotional development of children.

What You Need to Know

After you read this section you should be able to:
- Explore the impact of poverty on the cognitive and socioemotional development of young children in the United States.
- Describe how a child's neigborhood impacts school readiness.
- Describe examples of good child-care strategies, from family day care to day-care centers and government-sponsored programs, including Early Head Start.
- Describe how day care impacts cognitive and socioemotional development.

Testing Your Knowledge

The objectives addressed in this section may help you solve problems or understand situations such as those presented in the questions below. At the end of this section, with the knowledge you acquire, you should be able to respond to the following questions in writing. Answer guides are given at the end of this chapter.

1. A couple you know has to send their child to day care because they both have to to work to make ends meet. What can you tell them about their options, the effects of day care on children, and the state of the day care industry?

2. You overhear your uncle say that programs like Head Start and Early Head Start are just glorified baby-sitting services and he doesn't want his tax money paying for such programs. Counter his statement with what you know about the benefits of these programs and the consequences of not having such programs.

Toddlerhood: Age of Autonomy *and* Shame and Doubt (pages 129–134)

What It's All About

Two-year-olds start to develop self-conscious emotions. They are capable of feeling pride, shame, and guilt. Two-year-olds are learning to connect with other children and socialize. Since they are running around and can get into more trouble and create more mess, their parents want more compliance from them. There are more rules to follow. At this age we also begin to see a real difference in the exuberant and shy child. With both the overly shy and the exuberant child, the parents need a strong attachment and they need to adapt to fit the child's needs in a sensitive and loving way. In this section, we will discuss the emerging self and its effects on the child's environment.

What You Need to Know

After you read this section you should be able to:

- Identify the task of toddlers (1 to 2 years old) in terms of Erikson's task of autonomy versus shame and doubt.
- Discuss the socialization process of toddlers and the relationship of the self-conscious emotions to this concept.
- Identify possible outcomes for shy and exuberant toddlers.
- Explain the long-term consequences of various attachment styles, including effects of power assertion and striving for a goodness of fit for an individual child.

Testing Your Knowledge

The objectives addressed in this section may help you solve problems or understand situations such as those presented in the questions that follow. At the end of this section, with the knowledge you acquire, you should be able to respond to the following questions in writing. Answer guides are given at the end of this chapter.

1. A friend's baby fusses at every little change in life. What kind of baby might this be, and what is the best way to raise this kind of child?

2. Your nephew is almost 2 years old, and your brother wonders if he has ADHD because he doesn't seem to listen and doesn't want to share with other children. Offer your brother some reassurance by explaining how your nephew's behavior is normal, and explain the challenges of socializing a child of this age. Address the issue of temperament in your explanation.

Put It All Together

Matching Items

Match the appropriate term with its definition or description. Answers appear at the end of the chapter

_____1. when a child checks to get guidance

_____2. connection to a caregiver

_____3. a baby's reflexive behavior that elicits pleasure in adults

_____4. caregiver departure creates upset baby

_____5. method of testing attachment styles

_____6. becoming aware of your own individuality

_____7. a person's manner of thinking and behaving

_____8. caretaker and infant are attuned to one another

_____9. teaching one to obey society's norms

_____10. when environment is correct for temperament

_____11. joyful response when reunited with parent

_____12. freezing or fear when reunited with parent

A.   goodness of fit
B.   secure attachment
C.   synchrony
D.   social smile
E.   socialization
F.   disorganized attachment
G.   attachment
H.   social referencing
I.   temperament
J.   Strange Situation
K.   separation anxiety
L.   autonomy

Multiple-Choice Questions

Circle the best answer for each question. Answers appear at the end of the chapter.

1. Around 2 months of age which of the following first develops?
    A. the social smile
    B. attachment in the making
    C. clear-cut attachment
    D. hearing

2. Around 4 months of age which of the following first develops?
    A. the social smile
    B. attachment in the making
    C. clear-cut attachment
    D. hearing

3. Around 7 or 8 months of age which of the following first develops?
    A. the social smile
    B. attachment in the making
    C. clear-cut attachment
    D. hearing

4. If a baby is adopted before _____ months of age he/she is unlikely to have developmental problems.
    A. 4
    B. 6
    C. 12
    D. 24

5. These children rarely show signs of separation anxiety and seem unreactive.
    A. avoidant attached
    B. anxious-ambivalent attached
    C. disorganized attached
    D. securely attached

6. These children are clingy and overly nervous.
    A. avoidant attached
    B. anxious-ambivalent attached
    C. disorganized attached
    D. securely attached

7. Poverty affects which of the following?
    A. high school graduation rates
    B. stress levels
    C. temperamentt
    D. All of the above.

8. Which of the following is most important regarding child care and development?
    A. high-quality preschool
    B. income level
    C. stimulating home life
    D. stimulating home and school life

9. Child care includes which of the following?
    A. a relative cares for the child
    B. a nanny cares for the child
    C. The child is placed in a center specifically for child care.
    D. All of the above.

10. Erikson's challenge during toddlerhood is which of the following?
    A. basic trust versus mistrust
    B. initiative versus guilt
    C. autonomy versus shame and doubt
    D. industry versus inferiority

11. When our survival is threatened, we may engage in _____ regardless of our age.
    A. proximity seeking behavior
    B. autonomous behavior
    C. power assertion
    D. stranger anxiety

12. Jade is 4 years old and though she prefers to be with her mother, she is able to say good-bye to her without suffering from a great deal of anxiety. According to Bowlby, Jade has developed a _____ of attachment.
    A. disorganized model
    B. self-conscious model
    C. working model
    D. insecure model

13. Parents with exuberant toddlers may be tempted to engage in:
    A. synchrony.
    B. power assertion.
    C. socialization.
    D. proximity seeking behavior.

14. Lila has accidentally broken a coffee mug. If Lila hangs her head and begins to whimper, then we can assume that she has acquired:
    A. autonomy.
    B. self-conscious emotions.
    C. attachment.
    D. social referencing.

Short-Answer and Essay Question

Write a few sentences in the space below the question. For longer answers, jot down the points you want to make. Organize your ideas in an outline or other graphic method. Then, write the full essay on a separate piece of paper.

1. Explain attachment. In your answer list the styles of attachment, give examples of behavior associated with each style, and explain the research method used to evaluate a child's attachment.

Answer Key to Chapter 4

Matching Items

1.	H	7.	I
2.	G	8.	C
3.	D	9.	E
4.	K	10.	A
5.	J	11.	B
6.	L	12.	F

Multiple-Choice Items

1.	A	8.	D
2.	B	9.	D
3.	C	10.	C
4.	B	11.	A
5.	A	12.	C
6.	B	13.	B
7.	C	14.	B

Short-Answer and Essay Question

1. **Question:** Explain attachment. In your answer list the styles of attachment, give examples of behavior associated with each style, and explain the research method used to evaluate a child's attachment.

   Answer guide: Did you notice all the parts of this question? Did you include secure and insecure attachment in your answer? Insecure attachment can be broken into other parts; did you include those? A complete answer would also describe the difference between the types of insecure attachment. You also need to explain the Strange Situation. Your explanation should include the name of the psychologist who invented the Strange Situation as well as the procedure used. Your answer should not be limited by the attachment styles. In an explanation of attachment you should include information about Harry Harlow and his experiments. Did you include the effects of stress on attachment and the role attachment plays in later life?

Testing Your Knowledge

Attachment: The Basic Life Bond

1. **Question:** Your friend has a 3-week-old baby and says she feels like all she does is feed the baby, change her diapers, respond to her cries, and do laundry. She also does all of this in a fog because of her sleep deprivation. She wonders if her baby even knows or cares who is doing these things for her. In order to reassure your friend, you want to describe the attachment response and the ensuing dance between child and caregiver. What kinds of things will you tell her?

   Answer guide: In your response you would want to describe the preattachment phase (which is the stage the baby is in now), the social smile and its rewards, attachment in the making, and clear-cut attachment. You should also discuss the possible development of stranger and separation anxiety, social referencing, and synchrony.

Settings for Development

1. **Question:** A couple you know has to send their child to day care because they both have to work to make ends meet. What can you tell them about their options, the effects of day care on children, and the state of the day-care industry?

   Answer guide: There is a difference between family care and day care. Did you consider that in your answer? What does the book say about attachment and day care? Effects of day care vary depending on the quality of care. Did you discuss quality issues in your answer? Add some data they should look for when comparing day-care quality. Quality varies dramatically in the United States; better and worse in other countries. Did you assume that this couple lived in the United States? What if they were in a different country?

2. **Question:** You overhear your uncle say that programs like Head Start and Early Head Start are just glorified baby-sitting services and he doesn't want his tax money paying for such programs. Counter his statement with what you know about the benefits of these programs and the consequences of not having such programs.

   Answer guide: Be sure to describe both Early Head Start and Head Start and the effectiveness of these programs. You should also describe the impact of poverty on development including the impact on academics, health, and lack of stimulation.

Toddlerhood: Age of Autonomy and Shame and Doubt

1. **Question:** A friend's baby fusses at every little change in life. What kind of baby might this be, and what is the best way to raise this kind of child?

   Answer guide: The baby could be shy and inhibited. What are the socializing characteristics of this kind of child? Did you include a reference to the biology of this type of child? What are the expectations as this type of child ages? Did you include information about exposing the child to the environment? Did you talk about the goodness of fit in your answer? Did you talk about empathic, secure, loving attachments?

2. **Question:** Your nephew is almost 2 years old, and your brother wonders if he has ADHD because he doesn't seem to listen and doesn't want to share with other children. Offer your brother some reassurance by explaining how your nephew's behavior is normal, and explain the challenges of socializing a child of this age. Address the issue of temperament in your explanation.

   Answer guide: Explain to your brother the challenges of socializing such a young child and what problems most parents see in young children. You should also point out that your nephew may have a naturally exuberant temperament and that it is important to find a good temperament-socialization fit.

Chapter 5

Physical and Cognitive Development

Do you wish you could go back to your childhood? Was your childhood a time of laughter and joy with someone to care for you? Was it full of unconditional love without any worries? Or is your childhood something to forget? Do you remember struggling to find food and proper housing with divorced or arguing parents? Was your childhood full of sickness and stress, or was it healthy and stress-free? Wouldn't it be great if childhood could be loving and free of mental and physical stress for everyone? In this chapter we will discuss the factors that influence physical and cognitive development of children from ages 3 to 11.

Our childhood is one of the longest of the animal species. Relatively speaking, the longer the life of a mammal, the longer is its age before sexual maturity. Why does it take so long to get to adolescence? Three-year-olds are little adults, with none of the necessary self-regulation that takes years to develop. At age 3, there are peculiar thoughts going through their brains and the world is full of absolutes. There will be major cognitive advances that will occur in specific patterns throughout childhood. These changes take time.

Spectacular changes in language and physical development will also take place. By the age of 3, children have a grasp on speech, but there is a lot more they will have to learn to become proficient at their culture's language. Children are good at running around by 3 years of age, and they need practice to hone their physical skills. It takes time to develop the precision of perfection.

Setting the Context (pages 142–143)

What It's All About

Why do we need childhood? The social answer is that we live in a structured society that requires us to develop math, language, and social skills. We need time to learn the very basic skills which we will build upon to get a job to support ourselves and our families and to maintain more than a subsistence level society. It takes time before we can control impulsive behavior, reason through problems, and develop decision making skills. Biologically speaking, we grow slowly. The frontal lobes of the brain are responsible for many behaviors we consider mature. That area of the brain does not enter the pruning phase until 9 years of age. In this section we will discuss some of the special learning tasks of childhood and take a closer look at the brain.

What You Need to Know

After you read this section you should be able to:

- Understand the role of early and middle childhood as a time when humans master the rules of living in society, absorb lessons from previous generations, and fine-tune the ability to understand the intentions of others.

• Discuss the development to maturity of the frontal lobes, which are involved in higher reasoning and planning.

Testing Your Knowledge

The objectives addressed in this section may help you solve problems or understand situations such as that presented in the question below. At the end of this section, with the knowledge you acquire, you should be able to respond to the following question in writing. Answer guides are given at the end of this chapter.

1. Humans take longer to mature than other species. This is because of the social tasks that we must learn. Explain what these social tasks are and describe the corresponding changes that occur in the brain.

Physical Development (pages 143–148)

What It's All About

In addition to changes in the brain, 3- to 7-year-olds show dramatic changes in physical growth and development in both fine and gross motor skills. It's not possible to train children to perform tasks beyond their abilities, but parents and teachers can ensure that children experience a good person-environment fit that provides age-appropriate activities and challenges. In many developing countries, physical abilities may be impacted by undernutrition, while in developed countries like the United States the problem is at the opposite end of the continuum—obesity. In this section, you will learn about changes in motor skills, threats to motor skill development, the extent of the obesity problem in the United States, and how parents and teachers can help overweight and obese children achieve optimal development.

What You Need to Know

After you read this section you should be able to:

• Understand the process of physical development from toddlerhood to middle childhood, and identify milestones in gross and fine motor skills.

• Explain the influence of environmental factors, especially undernutrition, on the physical development of children.

• Describe the prevalence of childhood obesity, its causes, and ways in which it threatens the development and health of children.

Testing Your Knowledge

The objectives addressed in this section may help you solve problems or understand situations such as that presented in the question below. At the end of this section, with the knowledge you acquire, you should be able to respond to the following question in writing. Answer guides are given at the end of this chapter.

1. Someone you know is worried about their child's physical development. What environmental factors should they control to optimize their child's physical growth?

Cognitive Development (pages 148–162)

What It's All About

Why is the sky blue? Because blue is my favorite color. That's the response you may get from a 4-year-old. Ask a 10-year-old and he/she may tell you what was taught in science class about light waves and gas molecules. How do children of different ages understand the world? Jean Piaget was interested in these qualitative differences and he proposed a stage theory of cognition to explain them. Young children are in the preoperational stage and older children are in the concrete operations stage. According to Piaget, some internal mechanism leads to the shift from one stage to another. Lev Vygotsky, a Russian psychologist, proposed that children are apprentices in thinking, and social interactions with others drive our cognitive development. Information-processing theory provides yet another approach to examining cognitive development, and in this section you will see how information-processing theory can be applied to children with attention deficit/hyperactivity disorder.

What You Need to Know

After you read this section you should be able to:

- Present Piaget's cognitive stages of preoperational and concrete operational thinking.
- Understand that all children progress from preoperational to concrete operational thinking, but the age at which children transition from phase to phase may differ, depending on their culture.
- Describe criticisms of Piaget's ideas about cognitive development in children.
- Present Lev Vygotsky's concept of zone of proximal development and use of scaffolding in which learning occurs as adults tailor instructions to a child's abilities.
- Describe the processes of memory and executive functions using the information-processing model.
- Present the definition, and then explain the potential causes and treatments of attention deficit/ hyperactivity disorder (ADHD).

Testing Your Knowledge

The objectives addressed in this section may help you solve problems or understand situations such as those presented in the questions below. At the end of this section, with the knowledge you acquire, you should be able to respond to the following questions in writing. Answer guides are given at the end of this chapter.

1. A friend has a child diagnosed with ADHD. What are some interventions he can use to help the child cope?

2. A child asks her father to turn out the lights and then to turn off the sun. In which of Piaget's stages is this child? What other concepts will this child find hard to understand?

3. Naomi wants to teach her granddaughter, Allia, how to bake. Use Vygotsky's ideas to describe how Naomi can effectively scaffold this task for her granddaughter.

Language (pages 162–164)

What It's All About

Wow! What a spectacular, remarkable, and seemingly impossible amount of growth occurs in language skills from ages 1 to 6. Children learn and correctly use over 10,000 words in just 5 short years! That's five new words every single day. How do they do it? Chomsky says it must be part of our genetics. We must be programmed to learn language. We will see in this section that there is also some nurturing involved. We need practice and a scaffolder, as indicated by the terrible example of Genie.* MIT is currently conducting the Human Speechome Project,** a video recording the life of an infant exploring language acquisition. In this section, we will discuss some of the parts of speech and language. We will also discuss some of the stages of speech development and a little of the theory behind the acquisition of speech and language.

*For more information on Genie, go to
http://www.pbs.org/wgbh/nova/transcripts/2112gchild.html
** For more information on the Human Speechome Project, visit
www.media.mit.edu/cogmac/projects/hsp.html

What You Need to Know

After you read this section you should be able to:

- Understand Vygotsky's theory of inner speech.
- Discuss the development of adult language skills (phonemes, morphemes, syntax, and semantics).
- Describe the language errors of overregularization, overextension, and underextension.

Testing Your Knowledge

The objectives addressed in this section may help you solve problems or understand situations such as those presented in the questions that follow. At the end of this section, with the knowledge you acquire, you should be able to respond to the following questions in writing. Answer guides are given at the end of this chapter.

1. An acquaintance is worried because her daughter seems to talk to herself and give herself instructions. Explain this behavior from what you have learned in this section.

2. Your 3-year-old niece often expresses her wishes by saying, "Me want…" Why should you not be concerned about this behavior? When should you become concerned?

Specific Social Cognitive Skills (pages 164–169)

What It's All About

René Descartes said, "I think, therefore I am." Not only did he recognize thought, he attributed it to life. Children tend to attribute thinking and living to everything animate and otherwise, and at 3 years of age, everything thinks the same way. Everyone, and everything, has the same thoughts. There is little separation of individual minds. Developing an understanding of other minds and the intentions of others is important to surviving in any society. Children are able to develop this skill by 4 years of age. We are also able to accumulate and retrieve a vast storehouse of episodic memories. This gives us a rich history of our personal lives. Maybe that's why time seems to move faster in later years. Each year is an ever smaller percentage of our entire life. In this section, we will discuss autobiographical memories and the theory of mind.

What You Need to Know

After you read this section you should be able to:

- Explain how we develop autobiographical memories.
- Explain theory of mind as a child's knowledge of other people's perspectives, and point out that children with autism have special trouble mastering theory-of-mind tasks.

Testing Your Knowledge

The objectives addressed in this section may help you solve problems or understand situations such as those presented in the questions below. At the end of this section, with the knowledge you acquire, you should be able to respond to the following questions in writing. Answer guides are given at the end of this chapter.

1. A friend just came back from a trip to Asia. In what way can she build her child's memories of this trip according to this section's material?

2. Find someone with a young child (2 to 5 years of age) and complete the false-belief task on page 166 of your textbook. Record your results.

Put It All Together

Matching Items

Match the appropriate term with its definition or description. Answers appear at the end of the chapter.

_____1. recognizing object equality when shape changes

_____2. ordering according to some property

_____3. knowing your own mental state and no one else's

_____4. the sounds of speech

_____5. the smallest unit of meaning

_____6. not using the irregular verb

_____7. calling all four-legged animals dogs

_____8. inability to think conceptually

_____9. fixing on one aspect of a substance

_____10. where cognitive action takes place

_____11. beginning of adult-like thinking

_____12. personal life history

A. phonemes
B. preoperations
C. overextensions
D. egocentrism
E. concrete operations
F. centering
G. overregularization
H. working memory
I. conservation
J. autobiographical memory
K. seriation
L. morphemes

Multiple-Choice Questions

Circle the best answer for each question. Answers appear at the end of the chapter.

1. What is it that evolutionary psychologists believe makes us special?
   A. grasping objects with our hands
   B. grasping the intentions of others
   C. using an opposable thumb
   D. communicating

2. What part of the brain helps us to reason?
   A. occipital lobes
   B. parietal lobes
   C. frontal lobes
   D. temporal lobes

3. Three-year-olds have trouble controlling their behavior because of what?
   A. too much sugar in their food
   B. not enough parental guidance
   C. slow growing frontal lobes
   D. None of the above.

4. Which of the following is NOT an example of a gross motor skill?
   A. jumping
   B. running
   C. tumbling
   D. writing

5. Which of the following does NOT cause growth to slow down?
   A. obesity
   B. abuse
   C. stress
   D. undernourishment

6. Which of the following is NOT a predictor of obesity?
   A. less gym hours in school
   B. less play outside
   C. more time spent watching TV
   D. nutrient-rich low-calorie food

7. What is it that causes a child to imagine a smashed ball of clay being made into a ball again?
   A. conservation
   B. serialization
   C. reversibility
   D. class inclusion

8. What is it called when a child consistently believes that their stuffed animals are alive?
   A. centering
   B. identity constancy
   C. animism
   D. artificialism

9. According to Vygotsky, we learn in the zone of proximal development by:
   A. bricking.
   B. roofing.
   C. mortaring.
   D. scaffolding.

10. A teacher discovers what a student can do and tailors her instruction a step ahead to push the student to learn something new. This teacher is using a method proposed by which of the following?
    A. Vygotsky
    B. Piaget
    C. Erikson
    D. Lorenz

11. Syntax is to _____ as semantics is to _____.
    A. morpheme; phoneme
    B. phoneme; morpheme
    C. meaning; structure
    D. structure; meaning

12. Your nephew and your sister watch as you hide a toy in a drawer. After your sister leaves the room you take the toy from the drawer and put it in the closet. Then you ask your nephew "When mommy comes back in, where will she think the toy is hidden?" If your nephew has developed theory of mind, then he will say:
    A. "In the closet."
    B. "In the drawer."
    C. "Under the bed."
    D. "I don't know."

13. Rehearsal, selective attention, and inhibition are all processes that are part of:
    A. executive functions.
    B. working memory.
    C. autobiographical memory.
    D. theory of mind.

14. Which of the following has NOT been implicated as a risk factor for ADHD?
    A. obesity
    B. prenatal smoking
    C. genetics
    D. environmental toxins

Short-Answer and Essay Question

Write a few sentences in the space below the question. For longer answers, jot down the points you want to make. Organize your ideas in an outline or other graphic method. Then, write the full essay on a separate piece of paper.

1. Compare and contrast the approaches of Piaget and Vygotsky.

Answer Key to Chapter 5

Matching Items

1. I	7. C
2. K	8. B
3. D	9. F
4. A	10. H
5. L	11. E
6. G	12. J

Multiple-Choice Questions

1. B	8. C
2. C	9. D
3. C	10. A
4. D	11. D
5. A	12. B
6. D	13. A
7. C	14. A

Short-Answer and Essay Question

1. **Question:** Compare and contrast the approaches of Piaget and Vygotsky.
   Answer guide: Both looked at cognitive development. Piaget had a stage approach and Vygotsky did not. Piaget focused on the role of the individual in bringing about developmental changes while Vygotsky focused on the role of others in mentoring cognitive development.

Testing Your Knowledge

Setting the Context

1. **Question:** Humans take longer to mature than other species. This is because of the social tasks that we must learn. Explain what these social tasks are and describe the corresponding changes that occur in the brain.
   Answer guide: You should describe the social tasks of learning the rules of our culture: learning how to take the perspectives of others and learning language.

In order to engage in these social tasks, we must also have more well-developed frontal lobes. Experience and maturation both lead to the development of connections in this area.

Physical Development

1. **Question:** Someone you know is worried about their child's physical development. What environmental factors should they control to optimize their child's physical growth?
   Answer guide: Development requires proper nutrition. Did you assume this person was in the United States? What if they were in another country? You should consider the possibilities that there is an inordinate amount of stress or possible abuse in the child's life. Did you consider the problem of obesity and its causes in your answer? What kind of exercise and training did you discuss for the child's developing skills?

Cognitive Development

1. **Question:** A friend has a child diagnosed with ADHD. What are some interventions he can use to help the child cope?
   Answer guide: One intervention is preparing the right person-environment fit. Don't ask children with ADHD to multitask. Environmental stimuli should be kept to a minimum. Reduce distractions and provide regular exercise routines. Don't use power assertion techniques. What kinds of drugs are available to relieve the symptoms of ADHD? Allocate an ADHD child's time for them.

2. **Question:** A child asks her father to turn out the lights and then to turn off the sun. In which of Piaget's stages is this child? What other concepts will this child find hard to understand?
   Answer guide: This child is in the preoperational stage of development. Define the stage. Do not simply list the components of the stage, such as animism, identity constancy, seriation, conservation, class

inclusion, reversibility, egocentric, selective attention, and theory of mind. Define each of these components as though the person reading the essay has no idea what the words mean.

3. **Question:** Naomi wants to teach her granddaughter, Allia, how to bake. Use Vygotsky's ideas to describe how Naomi can effectively scaffold this task for her granddaughter.

   Answer guide: Naomi should ensure that she has a secure relationship with her granddaughter. She should then start with a baking task that is relatively easy and fun. Perhaps, baking chocolate chip cookies would be a good start. She could have her granddaughter help her to measure out the ingredients and to help add them to the mix. Stirring in the chocolate chips may be too difficult but she could have her help add them and then spoon the batter on to a pan. She needs to give specific feedback and correct any mistakes in a sensitive way. The next time they bake, she could have her granddaughter try some steps on her own until she can gradually do the task with supervision and then independently.

Language

1. **Question:** An acquaintance is worried because her daughter seems to talk to herself and give herself instructions. Explain this behavior from what you have learned in this section.

   Answer guide: This behavior can be acceptable. Vygotsky called it self-talk. Self-talk is a form of self-scaffolding. Do not stop with the explanation of self-talk. Include the possible reasons why a child might self-talk. The demands placed on this child may be too great. Look at the child's life and consider reducing the demands slightly. Self-talk may give an adult insights into the child's inner mind.

2. **Question:** Your 3-year-old niece often expresses her wishes by saying, "Me want…." Why should you not be concerned about this behavior? When should you become concerned?

   Answer guide: Children of this age frequently use two morphemes to express themselves. By the time your niece is 4- or 5-years-old she should be constructing complete sentences and using "I" instead of "me."

Specific Social Cognitive Skills

1. **Question:** A friend just came back from a trip to Asia. In what way can she build her child's memories of this trip according to this section's material?

   Answer guide: In this essay you can discuss early childhood memories. How far back can a person remember? How old was this child? Discuss the progression of past-talk conversations. Discuss the differences in parental interactions with children and the outcomes of those differences. In your answer, include the cultural differences talked about in your text. Don't assume the friend and the child are from your own culture.

2. **Question:** Find someone with a young child (2 to 5 years of age) and complete the false-belief task on page 166 of your textbook. Record your results.

   Answer guide: If the child is 2- or 3-years-old, they would say that Ms. X will look for the toy under the bed because they have not yet developed theory of mind. Thus, they believe that Ms. X knows what they know. Children who are 4-years-old may exhibit the same behavior as a younger child or may have developed theory of mind, in which case they would say that Ms. X would look in the drawer. Five-year-olds should have developed theory of mind.

Chapter 6

Socioemotional Development

As you have already learned, we are each born with a temperament that is then shaped by our experiences and by the people around us. Do you remember the shy girl in third grade or the neighborhood bully? What about the boy in fifth grade who was always the first to befriend the new kid? In this chapter you will learn about the forces that help shape us to be outgoing or shy, helpful or aggressive, to feel good about ourselves or to lack self-confidence. You will also learn about the different ways in which children play and form friendships and how our culture and our gender contribute to our socioemotional development.

Setting the Challenge (page 174)

What It's All About

As children move into early childhood, they need to develop the ability to regulate their emotions. Most children are able to learn this skill but some children face challenges and develop internalizing tendencies, which lead them to act in an anxious and self-conscious manner, while other children may develop externalizing tendencies, which lead them to act in an impulsive and disruptive manner. In this introductory section, you will learn to distinguish these two tendencies.

What You Need to Know

After you read this section you should be able to:
- Understand that as children learn emotion regulation, they may exhibit either external tendencies, such as a form of aggression, or internal tendencies, such as anxiety.

Testing Your Knowledge

The objectives addressed in this section may help you solve problems or understand situations such as that presented in the question below. At the end of this section, with the knowledge you acquire, you should be able to respond to the following question in writing. Answer guides are given at the end of this chapter.

1. You are a teacher with two 7-year-old children in your class. Jane exhibits internalizing tendencies and Robby exhibits externalizing tendencies. The children are going to play on the playground for recess. What types of behavior do you expect from Jane, and what types of behavior do you expect from Robby?

Personality (pages 174–187)

What It's All About

Once we acquire the skill of seriation we begin to compare ourselves to others. Who is the tallest? Who is the prettiest? Who is the fastest runner? When we look to see how we stack up against others, we may begin to feel better or worse about ourselves. This sense of self-esteem becomes a major issue in childhood. If we see only our successes and don't acknowledge our failures, we may develop an unrealistic sense of high self-worth. If we are overly critical and feel powerless, then we may develop learned helplessness. In order to understand personality, it is also important to understand prosocial behaviors, which center on feelings of empathy, sympathy, shame, and guilt. Our culture reflects our feelings about prosocial acts and aggressive acts. Aggression comes in many forms and is shaped by gender. Some children are more prone to aggression and need special care during the early years. In this section, you will learn about self-esteem, prosocial behaviors, and aggression, as well as how parents and teachers can promote prosocial behavior, promote realistic self-esteem in children, and decrease problems associated with aggression.

What You Need to Know

After you read this section you should be able to:

- Explain that changes in self-awareness, which may influence a child's self-perception and self-esteem, are hallmarks of the transition to middle childhood.
- Connect Erikson's terms **industry** and **inferiority**, and describe the challenges of middle childhood.
- Explore how internalizing tendencies may lead to low self-esteem and a feeling of incompetence, known as learned helplessness.
- Discuss how to increase self-esteem through enhanced self-efficacy.
- Explore how praise can have negative effects on the self-efficacy of Black children.
- Discuss helpful, caring acts of prosocial behavior, including displays of altruism and empathy.
- Discuss induction as a strategy that teaches altruism by teaching a child who is hurtful towards others to recognize and understand the feelings of others.
- Distinguish between shame and guilt.
- Identify forms of aggression, including instrumental aggression (hurtful behavior a person initiates), reactive aggression (a response to being hurt), and relational aggression (aggression designed to damage social relationships).
- Define and explore reasons why highly aggressive children may experience the hostile attributional bias—a bias in which highly aggressive children feel that the world is out to get them.

Testing Your Knowledge

The objectives addressed in this section may help you solve problems or understand situations such as those presented in the questions below. At the end of this section, with the knowledge you acquire, you should be able to respond to the following questions in writing. Answer guides are given at the end of this chapter.

1. A mother you know has a child who is not physically fit, and the child is feeling bad about it. What can the mother do, aside from exercise and diet, to increase the child's self-esteem?

2. What can a parent do to increase prosocial behavior in a small child?

3. As children mature, the types of aggressive behaviors they show change. Describe the differences between a 3-year-old's aggressive behavior and an older child's aggressive behavior. Be sure to use the terminology used in your textbook.

Relationships (pages 187–198)

What It's All About

Play behavior shapes our ability to deal with the wider world. As children move from solitary play to collaborative play we see their social skills improve. When we are young we will play with almost anyone. Later we develop casual friendships and friendships of convenience. If we are lucky, we will have one or two very close friends. Popularity becomes important as we join the social scene, but some children never become part of the popular crowd. What does it take to make a friend or be a friend? How does one become popular or rejected? What makes a bully or a victim? You will learn about these issues in this section.

What You Need to Know

After you read this section you should be able to:

- Define different styles of play—from rough-and-tumble play to fantasy play and collaborative pretend play—and connect fantasy play to what Vygotsky believed was children's practice of adult roles.
- Explore the biological and socialized aspects of play based on gender schema theory in which recognition of one's sex determines model behaviors.
- Discuss relationships that children form based on their ability to regulate emotions and utilize social skills; point out the range from a popular child to a rejected child.
- Discuss the factors that make children vulnerable to bullying and how bullying is a normal part of growing up.
- Understand that prevention programs help to stop bullying and allow the social norms in a school to shift toward prosocial behavior.

Testing Your Knowledge

The objectives addressed in this section may help you solve problems or understand situations such as those presented in the questions below. At the end of this section, with the knowledge you acquire, you should be able to respond to the following questions in writing. Answer guides are given at the end of this chapter.

1. Play is fun, but what other purposes does it serve?

2. Someone you know blames the media and social pressures for the stereotypical way girls and boys play. What can you tell them to prove that there are other factors influencing children's play?

3. A child confides in you that he is being bullied at school. What are some of the interventions that can be used to decrease this problem?

Put It All Together

Matching Items

Match the appropriate term with its definition or description. Answers appear at the end of the chapter.

_____1. teaching empathy and guilt
_____2. feeling responsible
_____3. knowing you are a separate entity
_____4. good works done possibly seeking rewards
_____5. good works done without regard to self
_____6. hurting someone to get a toy
_____7. hurting someone because they hurt you
_____8. giving up without trying
_____9. everyone is out to get you
_____10. watching and modeling your own sex
_____11. hitting and shoving with no intent to harm
_____12. a pattern of bullying and being bullied

A. self-awareness
B. learned helplessness
C. altruism
D. instrumental aggression
E. hostile attributional bias
F. induction
G. gender schema theory
H. bully-victim
I. rough-and-tumble play
J. guilt
K. reactive aggression
L. prosocial

Multiple-Choice Questions

Circle the best answer for each question. Answers appear at the end of the chapter.

1. Which of the following describes a child who acts on his/her immediate emotions?
   A. externalizing
   B. internalizing
   C. inhibiting
   D. regulating

2. Which of the following describes a child who is timid and self-conscious?
   A. externalizing
   B. internalizing
   C. inhibiting
   D. regulating

3. Erikson's challenge during middle childhood is which of the following?
   A. basic trust versus mistrust
   B. initiative versus guilt
   C. autonomy versus shame and doubt
   D. industry versus inferiority

4. Children in this Eriksonian stage of development are testing their abilities in the world.
   A. basic trust versus mistrust
   B. initiative versus guilt
   C. autonomy versus shame and doubt
   D. industry versus inferiority

5. Which of the following is NOT one of the five basic competencies?
    A. scholastics
    B. athletics
    C. health maintenance
    D. physical appearance

6. Which of the following is NOT a characteristic of children with externalizing tendencies?
    A. tend to be highly self-critical
    B. read failure into neutral situations
    C. are at risk of developing learned helplessness
    D. All of the above.

7. A child who gives her favorite teddy bear to calm an upset friend is probably what age?
    A. 3
    B. 10
    C. 12
    D. None of the above.

8. What would define a person helping someone with the intention of getting something in exchange?
    A. altruism
    B. empathy
    C. sympathy
    D. prosocial

9. If you feel another person's emotions, what is that called?
    A. altruism
    B. empathy
    C. sympathy
    D. prosocial

10. Which of the following produces a feeling of humiliation?
    A. induction
    B. guilt
    C. shame
    D. None of the above.

11. Jenny purposefully invited all of Crystal's friends but not Crystal to her party, and made it clear that Crystal was not wanted. Which of the following forms of aggression is this?
    A. instrumental
    B. reactive
    C. relational
    D. direct

12. Which of the following forms of play is found fairly equally in both sexes?
    A. fantasy
    B. rough-and-tumble
    C. fighting
    D. wrestling

13. Which of the following forms of play is found mostly in girls?
    A. large groups
    B. collaborative
    C. rough-and-tumble
    D. running around

Short-Answer and Essay Questions

Write a few sentences in the space below the question. For longer answers, jot down the points you want to make. Organize your ideas in an outline or other graphic method. Then, write the full essay on a separate sheet of paper.

1. Discuss play. Include the different styles of play, gender differences, and some of its possible purposes and causes.

2. Think back to what you've learned so far about brain development, cognition, and psychosocial development from infancy through childhood. What are some reasons that very young children don't form friendships like those we see in middle childhood?

Answer Key to Chapter 6

Matching Items

1. F
2. J
3. A
4. L
5. C
6. D
7. K
8. B
9. E
10. G
11. I
12. H

Multiple-Choice Questions

1. A
2. B
3. D
4. B
5. C
6. D
7. A
8. D
9. B
10. C
11. C
12. A
13. B

Short-Answer and Essay Questions

1. **Question:** Discuss play. Include the different styles of play, gender differences, and some of its possible purposes and causes.
   Answer guide: Describe rough-and-tumble play and collaborative play. Discuss the differences in male and female play. Collaboration and heirarchical structures and the sizes of groups should be part of your gender discussion. Talk about exercise and obesity and fitness. Don't forget how children move from gross motor skills to fine motor control. Include the way play allows children to work out problems in their lives and how they can cement an understanding of the norms of their society.

2. **Question:** Think back to what you've learned so far about brain development, cognition, and psychosocial development from infancy through childhood. What are some reasons that very young children don't form friendships like those we see in middle childhood?
   Answer guide: Your answer should address the issues of self-awareness, egocentrism in preoperational thought, lack of seriation in preoperational thought (difficulty seeing similarities between ourselves and others, which is one of the main ways that we establish friendships), lack of behavioral self-control due to lack of frontal lobe development (this will increase physical aggression, which tends to decrease someone's desire to be your friend), and lack of prosocial behaviors, which promote a give-and-take behavior necessary for friendships.

Testing Your Knowledge

Setting the Challenge

1. **Question:** You are a teacher with two 7-year-old children in your class. Jane exhibits internalizing tendencies, and Robby exhibits externalizing tendencies. The children are going to play on the playground for recess. What types of behavior do you expect from Jane, and what types of behavior do you expect from Robby?
   Answer guide: Jane is likely to engage in a solitary activity or wait for others to ask her to join an activity. Robby will likely try to take over activities and perhaps have some disagreements, if not physical encounters, with others.

Personality

1. **Question:** A mother you know has a child who is not physically fit, and the child is feeling bad about it. What can the mother do, aside from exercise and diet, to increase the child's self-esteem?
   Answer guide: Friendships provide a cushion to children with low self-esteem. Your answer should also include the value of a secure loving relationship with the caregiver. The child's physical competency is only one of the five competencies. Your text gives some good advice about playing down the negatives and playing up the positives. Remember to include a phrase about the differences in other cultures.

Provide realistic feedback and help the child find other areas in which they excel.

2. **Question:** As children mature the types of aggressive behaviors they show change. Describe the differences between a 3-year-old's aggressive behavior and an older child's aggressive behavior. Be sure to use the terminology employed in your textbook.

   Answer guide: Young children are more likely to engage in physical aggression because they can't inhibit physical responses (remember the frontal lobes are still underdeveloped at this age). Young children's aggression is usually instrumental or reactive. As children mature and can engage in more planning behavior, aggression becomes more calculated, less physical, and often has the objective of hurting the other person's self-esteem (relational aggression).

Relationships

1. **Question:** Play is fun, but what other purposes does it serve?

   Answer guide: In addition to providing physical health benefits, play allows children to practice adult roles, gain a sense of control over their lives, and helps to teach social norms.

2. **Question:** Someone you know blames the media and social pressures for the stereotypical way girls and boys play. What can you tell them to prove that there are other factors influencing children's play?

   Answer guide: Describe the biological reasons for play and the role of the hormone testosterone. Explain the observational studies with male and female rhesus monkeys and the effects of injected testosterone on the play behavior of female rhesus monkeys. Research with humans includes correlational studies measuring the testosterone levels of women pregnant with female fetuses and the behavior of these fetuses as they developed into girls and young women.

3. **Question:** A child confides in you that he is being bullied at school. What are some of the interventions that can be used to decrease this problem?

   Answer guide: Unassertive and anxious children are vulnerable to bullying. Help the child to improve himself in these areas. Since bullying usually requires an audience, you'll need to address the other children in the class. In your answer describe the Olweus program. Discuss how parents may need to help an anxious child connect with playmates. Early intervention is the key to prevent both bullying and victimization.

Chapter 7

Settings for Development: Home and School

Families come in many varieties. Most children in the United States live in a home with two parents. Those parents may be their biological, step, or adoptive parents. The percentage of two-parent households has shown a steady decline over the past decade. The idea of a nuclear family consisting of two parents and their children may become a thing of the past in the next few decades. Currently, one-third of children in the United States live in single-parent homes (mostly with their mothers), with grandparents, with other relatives, or with nonrelatives. Psychologists must study these changes in family structures and how these changes may impact development. Family structure, parenting styles, culture, discipline, and child maltreatment are all subsumed under the heading of home in this chapter. Special attention will be paid to children and families who differ from the stereotypical nuclear family.

What about the impact of school on development? There is tremendous diversity in children's experiences in schools. Some schools are overcrowded and have few resources while others have optimal student-to-teacher ratios and have funding surpluses and model programs. Teachers and classrooms are pivotal in a child's learning experiences but what about other factors? In this chapter, you will learn about the influences of teachers and classrooms but also about the impact of factors such as poverty, intelligence, and learning disabilities.

Setting the Context (pages 204–205)

What It's All About

What is a home if not a family? What is a family? A strict definition would be a man and a woman with children they had together. That would leave out single mothers, parents with adopted children, foster families, blended families, grandparent households, and children living with same-sex couples. Homes in the United States are also diverse, with many households consisting of first- or second-generation immigrants.

What You Need to Know

After you read this section you should be able to:
- Understand the wide variety of types of families that exist in the United States today.
- Counter stereotypes about immigrants in the United States.

Testing Your Knowledge

The objectives addressed in this section may help you solve problems or understand situations such as that presented in the question below. At the end of this section, with the knowledge you acquire, you should be able to respond to the following question in writing. Answer guides are given at the end of this chapter.

1. Your friend contends that immigrants are "ruining" the United States. Use what you know about stereotypes regarding immigrants to counter his statement.

Home (pages 205–216)

What It's All About

No matter what kind of family a child lives in, the family's dynamic is drastically changed by death or divorce. The home includes sleeping arrangements, parenting and punishment styles, and possible child neglect or abuse. Environmental influences such as economics also play a role in the life of the home. We need all of these home variables in psychology.

What You Need to Know

After you read this section you should be able to:

*   Compare and contrast the four main parenting styles: authoritative, authoritarian, permissive, and rejecting-neglecting.
*   Explain the effects of parenting/child-rearing practices on children's development.
*   Discuss the qualities possessed by resilient children.
*   Understand the role of genes, peers, and parents in children's lives.
*   Present the pros and cons of corporal punishment, especially spanking.
*   Describe behaviors that constitute child maltreatment, and describe the classification of physical abuse, neglect, emotional abuse, and sexual abuse.
*   Understand the importance of parents' personalities, life stressors and children's vulnerabilities in abusive situations.
*   Explain the short-term and long-term impact of divorce on children

Testing Your Knowledge

The objectives addressed in this section may help you solve problems or understand situations such as that presented in the question below. At the end of this section, with the knowledge you acquire, you should be able to respond to the following question in writing. Answer guides are given at the end of this chapter.

1. Now that you have read the section, what were your parents' styles of parenting? Now that you know there are different styles, will you use the same style your parents used or try another approach? Why? Were you spanked? Will you (or have you) spank(ed) your children? Why or why not?

School (pages 216–230)

What It's All About

Schools have to find ways to place children in the proper learning environment. Some children are gifted, some are mentally challenged, and some have specific disabilities. Intelligence tests are used to find the proper placement for each child. The reliability and validity of these tests are often questioned. Intelligence itself is under scrutiny. How many types of intelligence are there? Intelligence also needs motivation, drive, and ambition as enablers. This section discusses some of these issues.

What You Need to Know

After you read this section you should be able to:

- Discuss the disparity between SES levels as it applies to children's performance in school.
- Describe the educational challenges of mental retardation and learning disabilities, especially dyslexia.
- Explain the meaning and interpretation of Wechsler's IQ scores.
- Describe the Flynn effect.
- Understand Charles Spearman's intelligence factor "g."
- Describe Sternberg's theory of successful intelligence.
- Present Gardner's multiple intelligences.
- Compare and contrast Wechsler's, Spearman's, Sternberg's, and Gardner's theories of intelligence.
- Describe a "successful" school.
- Differentiate between children who learn by intrinsic and extrinsic motivation.
- List and explain teaching strategies that promote relevance and interest, as well as foster relatedness and autonomy in students.

Testing Your Knowledge

The objectives addressed in this section may help you solve problems or understand situations such as those presented in the questions below. At the end of this section, with the knowledge you acquire, you should be able to respond to the following questions in writing. Answer guides are given at the end of this chapter.

1. A first-generation immigrant family has moved into the school district. You became friends with the family, even though there is a language barrier. What can you and the people of your community do to help their small children in the upcoming school year?

2. Your roommate took a standardized intelligence test in elementary school, and his score was in the average range. His brother's score got him placed in the gifted program. Your roommate is always putting himself down as the "not smart" one in the family. Your view of him, however, is that he is extremely gifted in music and that he always comes up with really interesting and unusual ideas. After reading your textbook, you have a clearer understanding of your roommate's intelligence. Tell him about the difference between traditional views of intelligence and the views of Gardner and Sternberg and how his intelligence may be categorized using these two theories.

Put It All Together

Matching Items

Match the appropriate term with its definition and description. Answers appear at the end of the chapter.

_____1. when a test gives consistent results

_____2. when a test measures what it set out to measure

_____3. test for measuring knowledge learned at school

_____4. increase in IQ scores over the last 100 years

_____5. motivation factor that comes from inside

_____6. type of intelligence for doing well on academic tests

_____7. a reading disability

_____8. motivation factor that comes from outside

_____9. type of intelligence for real-world competency

_____10. achieving an IQ score of 70 or below

_____11. purported to underlie performance on all intelligence tests

A. intrinsic
B. analytic
C. extrinsic
D. validity
E. reliability
F. dyslexia
G. MR
H. practical
I. achievement test
J. factor "g"
K. Flynn effect

Multiple-Choice Questions

Circle the best answer for each question. Answers appear at the end of the chapter.

1. Which of the following is a definition for a family?
   A. a married male and female who have children together
   B. two lesbians who adopt children
   C. a grandmother and her adopted grandchild
   D. All of the above.

2. Which of the following parenting styles reflects high on nurturing and low on rules?
   A. authoritarian
   B. authoritative
   C. permissive
   D. rejecting-neglecting

3. Which of the following parenting styles relates to high child achievement in academics and social skills?
   A. authoritarian
   B. authoritative
   C. permissive
   D. rejecting-neglecting

4. Which is NOT a quality of resilient children?
   A. introverted personality
   B. superior emotion-regulation
   C. one loving adult in their life
   D. a long form of the serotonin gene

5. Failure to provide adequate supervision and care is defined as which of the following?
    A. corporal punishment
    B. spanking
    C. physical abuse
    D. child neglect

6. Which of the following would define bodily injury that leaves bruises?
    A. corporal punishment
    B. spanking
    C. physical abuse
    D. child neglect

7. People who abuse their children often have which of the following characteristics?
    A. substance abuse
    B. depression
    C. angry temperament
    D. All of the above.

8. People who abuse their children are NOT likely to have which of the following?
    A. domestic violence
    B. severe poverty
    C. isolation
    D. elation

9. What child characteristic would put a child at risk of child abuse?
    A. crying excessively
    B. having a difficult temperament
    C. being an exuberant child
    D. All of the above.

10. Where do children of divorce have a statistical advantage?
    A. academics
    B. physical health
    C. mental health
    D. None of the above.

11. Which of the following is the latest test for child IQ?
    A. NEO PI
    B. WISC
    C. Factor "g"
    D. Stanford-Binet

12. Which of the following scores would rate a child as having a learning disability like dyslexia?
    A. 60
    B. 100
    C. 140
    D. None of the above.

13. Which of the following is an intelligence defined by Gardner?
    A. analytic
    B. dissociate
    C. autobiographical
    D. None of the above.

14. The observation that each successive generation of immigrant families blends in more with the American norm is a testament to the power of:
   A. analytic intelligence.
   B. acculturation.
   C. authoritative parenting.
   D. intrinsic motivation.

Short-Answer and Essay Questions

Write a few sentences in the space below the questions. For longer answers, jot down the points you want to make. Organize your ideas in an outline or other graphic method. Then, write the full essay on a separate piece of paper.

1. Discuss intelligence and achievement, and the new concepts of intelligence espoused by Gardner and Sternberg. Include a discussion of validity versus reliability.

2. Give a brief synopsis of the types of motivation. Include information and examples of the consequences of giving external rewards for performance and the consequences of reducing autonomy.

Answer Key for Chapter 7

Matching Items

1. E	7. J
2. F	8. I
3. H	9. C
4. B	10. K
5. A	11. D
6. G	

Multiple-Choice Questions

1. D	8. D
2. C	9. D
3. B	10. D
4. A	11. B
5. D	12. D
6. C	13. D
7. D	14. B

Short-Answer and Essay Questions

1. **Question:** Discuss intelligence and achievement and the new concepts of intelligence espoused by Gardner and Sternberg. Include a discussion of validity versus reliability.
   Answer guide: Intelligence is not easily defined. Students complain about how they freeze on achievement tests and don't show as much as they know. These tests are more achievement oriented. Freezing is part of the test. They measure exactly what they are supposed to measure—how well you will do in school. Your answer should also include the Gardner and Sternberg intelligences. A description of validity and reliability would also be appropriate.

2. **Question:** Give a brief synopsis of the types of motivation. Include information and examples of the consequences of giving external rewards for performance and the consequences of reducing autonomy.
   Answer guide: Intrinsic and extrinsic motivation should be described. Competition's effect on intrinsic motivation should be included. Since motivation decreases during the school years, it would be appropriate to include a discussion of the book's method of increasing motivation in school.

Testing Your Knowledge

Setting the Context

1. **Question:** Your friend contends that immigrants are "ruining" the United States. Use what you know about stereotypes regarding immigrants to counter his statement.
   Answer guide: Your answer should discuss the four stereotypes listed at the beginning of the chapter with appropriate statistical evidence to counter your friend's claim.

Home

1. **Question:** Now that you have read the section, what were your parents' styles of parenting? Now that you know there are different styles, will you use the same style your parents used or try another approach? Why? Were you spanked? Will you (or have you) spank(ed) your children? Why or why not?
   Answer guide: Describe the style that best fits your parents' styles and give examples of parental behavior that back up your interpretation of what style your parents used. Give reasons why you will use the style you chose and include outcomes from the research that back up your choice. Also describe the differing opinions on if and when to use spanking as a disciplinary technique.

School

1. **Question:** A first-generation immigrant family has moved into the school district. You became friends with the family, even though there is a language barrier. What can you and the people of your community do to help their small children in the upcoming school year?

Answer guide: If the parents cannot speak English, get tutors for the children and get the parents into an ESL program. Give some statistics on children with non–English-speaking parents. If the family is poor and living in poverty conditions, help out by donating textbooks and learning games to the family. Give some statistics on the effects of poverty on schoolchildren. There are immigrants who do not need help. Even with language problems, they prioritize school and their children do well. Do not assume in your answer that the children will have a problem. In your answer, do not assume that any problems which exist are because of their culture or language. Get the children and parents involved in the school programs. Get the children tested. They may be behind due to poverty and language, but they could also have learning challenges. The earlier these challenges are detected, the better the child will perform. Find the children's "Gardner" intelligence and help them find activities to express it.

2. **Question:** Your roommate took a standardized intelligence test in elementary school and his score was in the average range. His brother's score got him placed in the gifted program. Your roommate is always putting himself down as the "not smart" one in the family. Your view of him, however, is that he is extremely gifted in music and that he always comes up with really interesting and unusual ideas. After reading your textbook, you have a clearer understanding of your roommate's intelligence. Tell him about the difference between traditional views of intelligence and the views of Gardner and Sternberg and how his intelligence may be categorized using these two theories.

Answer guide: Describe Sternberg's factor "g" view of intelligence to him and then tell him how other researchers believe this is too narrow a view of intelligence. Both Gardner and Sternberg believe that we need to look at people's other gifts and talents. Your roommate would probably score high on Sternberg's creative intelligence and Gardner's musical intelligence.

Chapter 8

Physical Development

Most students reading this text are barely out of puberty while a small percentage can barely remember it. Most adults are happy to forget this awkward stage of life. The person in the mirror changes into a familiar, but strange, rendition of ourself. We become larger, hairier, and more awkward. Sexuality consumes our thoughts. Freud felt our sexual desires were caused by an internal drive. Although Freud called this drive "Eros," we now know that it is our hormones raging out of control. We have become capable of reproducing, but in many cultures and societies we are not allowed to do so. This chapter discusses our bodily changes during adolescence, the changes that occur in our self-concepts, and our sexuality.

Puberty (pages 238–250)

What It's All About

Sexual maturity: What's mature about it? Our bodies might be able to reproduce, but our minds are still immature. Who we are must be redefined and many of us are not prepared for the new classification of sexually mature adult. Psychologists and biologists study what causes the changes during puberty. They look for trends to determine the normal course of puberty. They also look for patterns in the ways that different cultures address this transitional period of life. In this section we will discuss the concepts of puberty.

What You Need to Know

After you read this section you should be able to:
- Understand the importance of culture and history when considering puberty as a rite of passage.
- Understand the secular trend in puberty in which menarche and spermarche occur at much younger ages, magnifying the gap between puberty and full adulthood.
- Differentiate between menarche and spermarche, including age of onset.
- Identify the hormonal changes of puberty that begin in middle childhood with the adrenal glands' production of adrenal androgens and continue with bodily changes, including the production of estrogens and testosterone.
- Describe the physical transition of young boys to young men and young girls to young women, in particular the appearance of primary and secondary sexual characteristics.
- Describe the differences in male and female puberty timetables.
- Discuss the implications for males and females of being either an early or a late maturer.

- Explain how predictions are made about whether or not a child will reach puberty at an early age.
- Explore ways that parents can help minimize an adolescent's puberty distress.

Testing Your Knowledge

The objectives addressed in this section may help you solve problems or understand situations such as those presented in the questions below. At the end of this section, with the knowledge you acquire, you should be able to respond to the following questions in writing. Answer guides are given at the end of this chapter.

1. Parents you know have a daughter who is maturing early. According to the book, what problems may this present for the child?
2. What can parents do to ease their child's transition from childhood to puberty?

Body Image Issues (pages 250–255)

What It's All About

As children we accept many different body types. As adults we may accept only Hollywood's current concept of beauty. If our body does not fit our image of beauty, we may be in for major lifetime disappointment. We can develop eating disorders and self-esteem issues. How we judge beauty can be influenced by our culture and race. How we view and deal with our bodies is the subject of this section.

What You Need to Know

After you read this section you should be able to:
- Describe the thin ideal.
- Explain eating disorders, and differentiate between anorexia nervosa and bulimia nervosa.
- Understand the factors that influence teens' distorted body images and the need to diet.
- Identify ways to improve a teenager's body image.

Testing Your Knowledge

The objectives addressed in this section may help you solve problems or understand situations such as those presented in the questions below. At the end of this section, with the knowledge you acquire, you should be able to respond to the following questions in writing. Answer guides are given at the end of this chapter.

1. Explain some of the biological and environmental factors that increase teens' preoccupation with their bodies.
2. A teenager you know is losing weight. What are the two main disorders discussed in the book that may be the cause?

Sexuality (pages 255–261)

What It's All About

Intercourse is not the only aspect of sexual behavior, but it is the one most talked about. Oral sex is still sex, that's why it's called "oral *sex*." Any contact with the reproductive organs or breasts is some form of sexual behavior. For females, reaching puberty early increases the chance of early sexual contact. Research shows that our first sexual thoughts can occur as early as age 10. Psychologists try to determine ways to predict sexual behavior and some of the results go against the general knowledge handed down by the previous generations. This section discusses the concepts surrounding sexuality.

What You Need to Know

After you read this section you should be able to:

- Recognize the pressing issue of human sexuality in adolescents' lives.
- Have a more accurate understanding of who is having intercourse during adolescence.
- Explain the sexual double standard (males versus females) and how recent research contradicts this standard.
- Understand how to design teenager-friendly sex education.

Testing Your Knowledge

The objectives addressed in this section may help you solve problems or understand situations such as those presented in the questions below. At the end of this section, with the knowledge you acquire, you should be able to respond to the following questions in writing. Answer guides are given at the end of this chapter.

1. A close family friend has a 15-year-old daughter. The parents are worried about sexual promiscuity. What does the book say about this issue?

2. Pretend that you are a high school teacher and your principal wants you to design the ideal sex education class for the tenth to twelfth graders in your school. What elements should you include?

Put It All Together

Matching Items

Match the appropriate term with its definition or description. Answers appear at the end of the chapter.

_____1. first menstruation
_____2. human sexual organs
_____3. male sexual organs
_____4. adrenal hormones
_____5. the hormonal axis of puberty
_____6. a mostly female hormone
_____7. a mostly male hormone
_____8. increases in height, weight, and muscle mass
_____9. more sexual freedom for boys and men
_____10. celebration of adolescence

A. gonads
B. HPG
C. puberty rite
D. estrogen
E. sexual double standard
F. menarche
G. testes
H. growth spurt
I. androgens
J. testosterone

Multiple-Choice Questions

Circle the best answer for each question. Answers appear at the end of the chapter.

1. On average, girls' breasts take how long to develop?
    A. 2 years
    B. 3 years
    C. 4 years
    D. 5 years

2. Early maturing girls tend to report which of the following?
   A. symptoms of distress
   B. sleep disorders
   C. a harmonious family life
   D. both A and B

3. What is the period called in which one achieves sexual maturity?
   A. adolescence
   B. pubescence
   C. puberty
   D. senescence

4. The average girl outwardly matures how many years before the average boy?
   A. 1 year
   B. 2 years
   C. 3 years
   D. 4 years

5. Our culture, which is media driven, pressures girls to lose weight. This is referred to as the:
   A. feminine ideal.
   B. feminine mystique.
   C. fashion model ideal.
   D. thin ideal.

6. What is the syndrome characterized by binging and purging called?
   A. anorexia
   B. bulimia
   C. obesity
   D. puberty

7. What do most parents worry about most when their daughter is an early maturing adolescent?
   A. homosexuality
   B. early heterosexual activity
   C. their daughter's physical prowess
   D. their daughter losing her friends

8. What has research shown us about a girl's first menstruation?
   A. Girls are reaching this time later in life.
   B. Stress postpones the onset of menarche.
   C. Weight gain delays the first menstruation.
   D. Heredity influences the timing.

9. Anorexia nervosa is an eating disorder that occurs most commonly in an individual at what percent of his or her ideal body weight or less?
   A. 120
   B. 90
   C. 85
   D. 65

10. Menarche and spermarche have been occurring at younger and younger ages. This finding is referred to as:
    A. a secular trend.
    B. the HPG axis.
    C. a puberty rite.
    D. a cross-sectional trend.

11. Physiological changes that are related directly to reproduction are referred to as:
     A. primary sex characteristics.
     B. secondary sex characteristics.
     C. tertiary sex characteristics.
     D. puberty.

12. Which of the following is NOT a transition to intercourse?
     A. having low SES
     B. being on a late puberty timetable
     C. being an African American male
     D. being female and having a risk-taking personality and low self-worth

Short-Answer and Essay Question

Write a few sentences in the space below the question. For longer answers, jot down the points you want to make. Organize your ideas in an outline or other graphic method. Then, write the full essay on a separate piece of paper.

1. What do the letters HPG stand for, and what sets off this developmental milestone?

Answer Key for Chapter 8

The following answers are the words you should have used to fill in the blanks for each of the sections above.

Matching Items

1. F	6. D
2. A	7. J
3. G	8. H
4. I	9. E
5. B	10. C

Multiple-Choice Questions

1. C	7. B
2. A	8. D
3. C	9. C
4. B	10. A
5. D	11. A
6. B	12. B

Short-Answer and Essay Questions

1. **Question:** What do the letters HPG stand for, and what sets off this developmental milestone?

   Answer guide: HPG stands for Hypothalamus, Pituitary, and Gonads. This is the group of anatomical structures that control the onset and development of puberty. Puberty and the HPG axis are initiated by the hypothalamic hormone that causes the pituitary to secrete its hormones. All of this in turn sends a message to the ovaries or testes to secrete their hormones, which begins puberty. Some triggers to this process that you should include in your answer are: healthy nutrition and normal weight gaining, calcification of the bones, and leptin production.

Testing Your Knowledge

Puberty

1. **Question:** Parents you know have a daughter who is maturing early. According

to the book, what problems may this present for the child?

   Answer guide: Did you consider that an early maturing child may be overweight? The extra weight may cause health problems in her adult years. Include a description of those possible weight issues. Early puberty increases such girls' popularity, anxiety, externalizing tendencies, acting-out behaviors, and high school drop-out rates. Their friends may include more older boys, which could in turn increase their own risky activities. For girls, early maturation can reduce overall adult height and increase the chance of pregnancy, depression, and a poor self-image. What type of school does their daughter attend? Does the school provide a nurturing authoritative environment?

2. **Question:** What can parents do to ease their child's transition from childhood to puberty?

   Answer guide: First and foremost, parents need to talk to their children. The talk should take place before the child is experiencing pubertal changes and should preferably be initiated by the same-sex parent. Parents may also want to consider their child's school situation. If possible, a parent could enroll a child in school with more intimate settings or a K-8 setting. Parents may also want to talk to their child's school principal about informative and appropriate sex education.

Body Image Issues

1. **Question:** Explain some of the biological and environmental factors that increase teens' preoccupation with their bodies.

   Answer guide: The main biological factor would be the impact of hormones. There are several environmental factors you could discuss including dating, peer pressure, and the influence of media.

2. **Question:** A teenager you know is losing weight. What are the two main disorders discussed in the book that may be the cause?
Answer guide: You should be discussing anorexia and bulimia in your answer. One in ten girls may have some symptoms of eating disorders. What are the rates of bulimia and anorexia? Are they increasing, decreasing, or remaining the same? Remember to include information about the roles of genetics, low self-efficacy, and reinforcement!

Sexuality

1. **Question:** A close family friend has a 15-year-old daughter. The parents are worried about sexual promiscuity. What does the book say about this issue?
Answer guide: The statistical trend shows that there isn't a lot to worry about. Only 10 percent of 15-year-olds are sexually active and more teens are using contraception. It doesn't mean parents should totally relax; they should still watch for signs of trouble. They need to worry if their daughter has friends that are sexually active. Her boyfriend's age and early puberty may be factors for concern. Poor socioeconomic status tends to favor promiscuity. TV viewing habits may lead to unrealistic expectations of behaviors. Personality factors like risk-taking and low self-worth are also predictors.

2. **Question:** Pretend that you are a high school teacher and your principal wants you to design the ideal sex education class for the tenth to twelfth graders in your school. What elements should you include?
Answer guide: Your answer will depend upon the type of group you envision (e.g., SES, ethnicity, etc.), but you should include the factors listed in Table 8.3 in the text and give examples of how these recommendations could be implemented.

Chapter 9

Cognitive and Socioemotional Development

Adolescent minds are a sometimes confusing mix of emotions and intelligence. Adolescents are on the verge of adult rational abstract thinking. However, their frontal lobes are developing too slowly to control their emotions. Their bodies are awash in hormones, which widely activate emotional responses. During the Great Depression in the United States, gangs of teenagers roamed the streets, and President Roosevelt's attempts to control these gangs via new laws also helped to shape adolescence into a defined life stage. Roosevelt's laws may have controlled the gangs in his time, but adolescence is all about congregating with friends. Thus, the influence of the social convoy is a favorite research topic of psychologists. This chapter discusses the mind of the adolescent and the need of adolescents to find a place among their peers.

Setting the Context (pages 266-267)

What It's All About

G. Stanley Hall first coined the term "storm and stress" to describe adolescence. Today, adolescence lasts much longer than it did during your grandparents' and great-grandparents' younger days. In this chapter, you will learn about the myths and stereotypes of adolescence, and you will learn how the adolescent mind and relationships with others are unique.

What You Need to Know

After you read this section you should be able to:

- Understand G. Stanley Hall's choice of the term "storm and stress" for the adolescent stage.
- Explain that adolescence did not become a life stage until the 1930s.
- Present accurate information regarding the stereotypes and myths about adolescents.

Testing Your Knowledge

The objectives addressed in this section may help you solve problems or understand situations such as that presented in the question below. At the end of this section, with the knowledge you acquire, you should be able to respond to the following question in writing. Answer guides are given at the end of this chapter.

1. Describe adolescence for a young woman who was a teenager in the United States in the 1920s and a young woman who was a teenager in the United States in the 1990s.

The Mysterious Teenage Mind (pages 267–286)

What It's All About

Teenagers are developing into adult thinkers. In many instances, they look, act, and sound like an adult . . . but a second later, that adult has vanished. They still retain aspects of their childhood patterns of thought, and this can cause issues with the adults around them and within themselves. They also have certain ways of thinking and their moral development continues to unfold. Adolescents are capable of both insightful thinking and irrational behavior. Teens believe they are invincible, the center of the world, and have a special relationship with an invisible audience that follows them everywhere. The changes occurring can be correlated to the development of their cortex and frontal lobes. The persons they become depend on their peers, family, and culture. This section discusses many of these issues.

What You Need to Know

After you read this section you should be able to:

- Explain the three main theories of teenage thinking/reasoning: Piaget's formal operational stage; Kohlberg's levels of moral development (preconventional, conventional, and postconventional); and Elkind's adolescent egocentrism, along with the imaginary audience and personal fable.

- Discuss the three aspects of "storm and stress" in adolescents' lives: social sensitivity, risk-taking, and emotionality.

- Explain that the experience-sampling technique has allowed researchers to learn that teens are more emotionally intense than adults, but not necessarily disturbed.

- Describe the academic, social, and economic costs of the drive for social status.

- Understand that teenagers' emotional intensity is associated with risk taking and non-suicidal injury in some teens.

- Highlight prior emotional problems (especially poor self-regulation), distance from family, and non-nurturing environments as causing a small minority of teenagers to get into serious trouble.

- Distinguish between adolescence-limited turmoil and life-course difficulties.

- Point out that brain development in the teen years contributes to making adolescence a dangerous life stage.

- Describe how society, including schools, can help to make the world a better fit for the teenage mind.

- Discuss the argument against the brain-deficit hypothesis (poor teen-society fit).

- Present tips to help parents bring out the best in their teenage children.

Testing Your Knowledge

The objectives addressed in this section may help you solve problems or understand situations such as those presented in the questions below. At the end of this section, with the knowledge you acquire, you should be able to respond to the following questions in writing. Answer guides are given at the end of this chapter.

1. A woman you know has a child entering the teenage years. She is afraid her child will become a delinquent. After reading this section, what can you tell her about this specific teenage pathway?

2. Max observes one of his classmates cheating. How might Max respond if he was exhibiting preconventional thinking? Conventional thinking? Postconventional thinking?

3. You teach seventh graders and notice one female student who is desperately trying to be popular. Why should you be concerned?

4. Provide some explanations for why teenagers engage in risk-taking activities.

Teenage Relationships (pages 286–293)

What It's All About

You can probably remember the groups of your peers that hung out together in high school. The jocks, popular kids, brains, delinquents, and many other social convoys can be found in most cultures around the world. While adolescents attempt to gain autonomy from family, they develop new relationships with their cohorts and end up creating different, and often closer, relationships with their parents. In their various crowds, they find people who share their values and goals. However, associating with the wrong crowds can be dangerous. This section deals with cliques, crowds, delinquency, alliances, and autonomy.

What You Need to Know

After you read this section you should be able to:

- Explain that mundane conflicts that arise between teenagers and their parents do not overwhelm the positive influence of family—especially of parents—on teenagers.

- Describe how immigrant children's experiences in establishing autonomy may differ, and discuss the influences of acculturation, peer group socialization, and the immigrant paradox.

- Recognize that peer groups, such as cliques and crowds, help prepare teenagers for later romantic involvement.

- Point out that those teenagers who belong to delinquent groups tend to have been unhappy before entering high school; delinquent groups, including gangs, encourage delinquent acts that foster antisocial and even criminal behaviors.

- Point out that adolescents in impoverished parts of the world are not always insulated from adult problems.

Testing Your Knowledge

The objectives addressed in this section may help you solve problems or understand situations such as that presented below. At the end of this section, with the knowledge you acquire, you should be able to respond to the following discussion topic in writing. Answer guides are given at the end of this chapter.

1. Describe some of the typical crowds of youth and discuss the term *deviancy training*.

Put It All Together

Matching Items

Match the appropriate term with its definition or description. Answers appear at the end of the chapter.

_____1. describing adolescence

_____2. Jean Piaget's final stage

_____3. capturing experiences of the moment

_____4. being antisocial into adult life

_____5. promoting self-efficacy in teenagers

_____6. a relatively large teenage peer group

_____7. antisocial behavior limited to teenage years

_____8. I am different from everyone else.

_____9. punishment and reward mentality

_____10. I am the center of your universe.

A. life course difficulties

B. sampling technique

C. preconventional morality

D. storm and stress

E. personal fable

F. a crowd

G. adolescent egocentrism

H. adolescence-limited turmoil

I. formal operational stage

J. youth developmental program

Multiple-Choice Questions

Circle the best answer for each question. Answers appear at the end of the chapter.

1. What are Kohlberg's three levels of moral judgment?
    A. preconventional, conventional, and postconventional
    B. preoperational, concrete operational, formal operational
    C. right, wrong, neutral
    D. generational, cultural, universal

2. _____ is the distorted feeling that one's own actions are the absolute center of everyone else's consciousness.
    A. Misplaced paranoia
    B. Adolescent egocentrism
    C. Acute identification
    D. Reserved personality

3. What factors can help a teenager thrive?
    A. social connectedness
    B. superior executive functions
    C. having a life interest
    D. All of the above.

4. A _____ is an intimate group with a membership of approximately six.
    A. social pairing
    B. peer collective
    C. clique
    D. crowd

5. _____ is the socialization of a young teenager into delinquency through conversations centered on performing antisocial acts.
    A. Gang reformation
    B. Deviancy training
    C. Youth development
    D. Storm and stress

6. Which of the following describes the range of adolescent emotions?
    A. Adolescents tend to have stable emotional feelings with few highs and lows.
    B. Adolescents tend to be depressed for no reason.
    C. Adolescents tend to react sharply to events causing their emotional balance to sway quickly between highs and lows.
    D. Adolescents tend to be emotionally disturbed.

7. Adolescent thinking is characterized by the ability to think:
    A. about possibilities and not just realities.
    B. about concepts presented in concrete terms.
    C. only about their own thoughts.
    D. All of the above.

8. Jan tells her mom that she cannot go to school today because she has a blemish on her face and everyone will stare at her. Jan is probably exhibiting which characteristic?
    A. the personal fable
    B. concrete thinking
    C. the imaginary audience
    D. storm and stress

9. Which of the following is NOT typical of gangs?
   A. They are predominantly groups of males.
   B. They are from high socioeconomic groups.
   C. They share a collective identity.
   D. They adopt certain symbols.

10. Immigrant teens may develop especially close relationships with their parents and outperform their peers academically despite stressors like poverty. This is refered to as the:
    A. acculturation paradox.
    B. immigrant paradox.
    C. peer socialization paradox.
    D. egocentric paradox.

Short-Answer and Essay Question

Write a few sentences in the space below the question. For longer answers, jot down the points you want to make. Organize your ideas in an outline or other graphic method. Then, write the full essay on a separate piece of paper.

1. Discuss some of the ways that we can help teenagers fit into the world, decreasing the risk of delinquent activity.

Answer Key for Chapter 9

Matching Items

1.	D	6.	F
2.	I	7.	H
3.	B	8.	E
4.	A	9.	C
5.	J	10.	G

Multiple-Choice Questions

1.	A	6.	C
2.	B	7.	A
3.	D	8.	C
4.	C	9.	B
5.	B	10.	B

Short-Answer and Essay Question

1. **Question:** Discuss some of the ways that we can help teenagers fit into the world, decreasing the risk of delinquent activity.
   Answer guide: In your answer, you should include the concept of prison sentences for teenagers as a rehabilitation lesson rather than strictly as punishment. You also should provide samples of ways to put distance between adult activities and teenage hormones in order to give the frontal lobe some time to develop. List a few enriching communal activities that provide a prosocial environment where teens can feel empowered and connected. Describe changes that can be made to high schools to give teens a better person–environment fit for their adolescent, off-rhythm, hormonally enriched brains.

Testing Your Knowledge

Setting the Context

1. **Question:** Describe adolescence for a young woman who was a teenager in the United States in the 1920s and a young woman who was a teenager in the United States in the 1990s.
   Answer guide: Your answer should include the fact that high school was not a requirement in the 1920s so a young woman who was a teen then may not have attended school beyond the seventh or eighth grade, depending on her socioeconomic status. You should also point out that there was no "teen culture" in the 1920s, so her world in her teen years would have been an adult world. She would have married early and moved from her parents' home to her own home. A teen in the 1990s would have been required to attend high school and probably graduated. She and her friends would have their own culture, and she probably would have attended college and delayed marriage and family until her mid- to late twenties.

The Mysterious Teenage Mind

1. **Question:** A woman you know has a child entering the teenage years. She is afraid her child will become a delinquent. After reading this section, what can you tell her about this specific teenage pathway?
   Answer guide: Does her child have good emotion regulation? Are the family relationships strong? How does that influence the child? Does the child have a life interest? What type of school does her child attend? Does it provide a nurturing environment, and is there a good person–environment fit for her child? Did you include information about authoritative parenting? Maybe the child will be delinquent in school, but does that mean he or she will be delinquent as an adult? Include a short description of adolescence-limited turmoil versus life-course difficulties. The parents can try to find and encourage prosocial friends and strong religious connections.

2. **Question:** Max observes one of his classmates cheating. How might Max respond if he was exhibiting preconventional thinking? Conventional thinking? Postconventional thinking?

   Answer guide: In preconventional morality, you might focus on Max's desire to avoid punishment or reap rewards. What would be the reward for turning in his classmate or not turning in his classmate? What would be punishing about the experience? For conventional thinking, focus on the rules related to behavior at school or rules regarding a student's role in the classroom. For postconventional thinking, focus on larger issues: Cheating in class is representative of what problem? How does this relate to larger moral issues?

3. **Question:** You teach seventh graders and notice one female student who is desperately trying to be popular. Why should you be concerned?

   Answer guide: The quest for popularity can have several negative consequences. Have the student's grades gotten worse? Are her peers isolating her or talking about her? Is she exhibiting externalizing tendencies? How is she emotionally? Does she appear to be depressed?

4. **Question:** Provide some explanations for why teenagesrs engage in risk-taking activities.

   Answer guide: There are several factors related to risk-taking behavior in adolescents. Adolescents' drive for social status may lead to acting out. Brain development is also implicated in risk-taking behavior. Did you discuss the development occurring in the frontal lobes and the influence of neurotransmitters? Additionally, our society may create a poor body-environment fit for individuals who are neither child nor adult.

Teenage Relationships

1. **Question:** Describe some of the typical crowds of youth, and discuss the term *deviancy training*.

   Answer guide: In your answer describe the need for teens to connect to their peers. You could include a comparison of cliques versus crowds. Then name some of the crowds and their specific function. For instance, one crowd in Western countries is called the jocks. The members of this crowd are the typical sports players at any high school. Finally, mention the "bad" crowd and how a teenager is ushered into this group by his or her own attributional bias. Describe the behavior of this crowd and how the members validate antisocial behavior through modeling, which we call deviancy training. Discuss the impacts of low socioeconomic status and bad economic conditions on gang development and the use of gang membership as protection.

Chapter 10

Constructing an Adult Life

If you are a traditional student reading this guide, then you are 17 to 20 years of age. You probably consider yourself an adult, but can you define what it means to be an adult? Do you have all the responsibilities of adulthood? Are you married? Do you have children, a career? Can you legally drink alcohol?

If you are an older student, you may be smiling at this point and thinking, "I remember when I was that age." Older students may remember wanting the responsibilities of an adult, but also wanting the freedom to enjoy a less responsible life for a little longer. These students probably were out from under their parents' control for the first time.

For some, this time of life is scary; for others, confusing; yet for others still, exhilarating. Can you relate?

The author of *Experiencing the Lifespan* defines adults as people that take responsibility for their actions, decide on their own values and beliefs, have an equal relationship with their parents, and provide for their own financial survival.

The events that usher in adulthood do not occur overnight. There is a transitional time between adolescence and adulthood during which we gradually grow into the responsibilities of adulthood. This chapter is about that in-between time—the time when we emerge into our adult selves.

In this chapter, you find out about some of the latest research in the field of emerging adulthood. You learn about issues that psychologists feel are important in the life of an emerging adult, including the college experience, finding a career, and finding love. You also discover why each person experiences this stage of life differently.

Emerging into Adulthood (pages 300–305)

What It's All About

We require a definition of adulthood before we can describe becoming one. For most people, becoming an adult is a gradual process. The definition of adulthood changes in different countries and cultures, so defining the emerging adult is a difficult process.

What You Need to Know

After you read this section you should be able to:
- Explain the importance of constructing an adult life.
- Understand the historical and cultural context that created the need to label emerging adulthood as a distinct phase of life.
- Describe the various features of emerging adulthood.

- Identify nest-leaving trends, and identify the main indicators of adulthood.
- Define the concept of the social clock, and understand the unique social-clock pressures that affect emerging adults.

Testing Your Knowledge

The objectives addressed in this section may help you solve problems or understand situations such as those presented in the questions below. At the end of this section, with the knowledge you acquire, you should be able to respond to the following questions in writing. Answer guides are given at the end of this chapter.

1. Imagine that you've made friends with an exchange student from Italy. How would your new friend view the experiences of 18- to 25-year-old Americans as similar or different to the experiences of Italians in the same age group?

2. Think about your own emerging progress toward adulthood. Would you rate yourself as "adult-like" in your progress toward a committed relationship, career, or financial independence? Are there differences in your levels of progress in these areas? How does this compare to the information in the textbook?

3. What is the social clock? In what ways are you "on-time" and in what ways are you "off-time"?

Constructing an Identity (pages 305–309)

What It's All About

Each emerging adult is unique. Each emerging adult is also in a constant state of change. Our life situations and our ethnic identities help to shape who we will become. In this section, you will learn how developmentalists approach the topic of identity.

What You Need to Know

After you read this section you should be able to:

- Discuss Erikson's work—for example, the quest for identity, identity confusion, and the period of moratorium.
- Understand Marcia's expansion of Erikson's concept of identity into four distinctive identity statuses: identity diffusion, identity foreclosure, moratorium, and identity achievement.
- Understand that emerging adults who are part of an ethnic minority may travel a different path as they search for their identities.

Testing Your Knowledge

The objectives addressed in this section may help you solve problems or understand situations such as that presented in the question below. At the end of this section, with the knowledge you acquire, you should be able to respond to the following question in writing. Answer guides are given at the end of this chapter.

1. You go home for vacation and your parents want to know why you haven't picked a major yet. What can you tell them about where you stand in the search for an identity? If you are a member of an ethnic minority, how might this impact your search for your identity?

Finding A Career (pages 309–316)

What It's All About

Some people go directly into the work force after high school. How do we choose a career that will be challenging and rewarding? How do we find a career that will provide us with a sense of flow? In the United States, many emerging adults choose a moratorium period and go to college. What predicts college success? How can college become a flow zone? In this section you will learn about the challenges of choosing a career, succeeding in college, and about the concept of flow.

What You Need to Know

After you read this section you should be able to:
- Explain the challenge of finding a career for emerging adults.
- Describe the concept of flow and its relationship to job satisfaction and intrinsic motivation.
- Compare and contrast the experiences of emerging adults who directly enter the work force versus those who go to college.
- Describe interventions for improving success in college completion and finding career identity.
- Explain how you can make college a flow zone.

Testing Your Knowledge

The objectives addressed in this section may help you solve problems or understand situations such as those presented in the questions that follow. At the end of this section, with the knowledge you acquire, you should be able to respond to the following questions in writing. Answer guides are given at the end of this chapter.

1. Your friends from high school are impressed that you are now a college student. They think you must have all the right answers. They want to know if they should attend your college or if they should even go to college. What will you tell them?

2. What are some experiences that leave you with a sense of flow? Compare what you are doing in college with the information in the Interventions section "Making College a Flow Zone" in your textbook. What changes can you make?

Finding Love (pages 316–326)

What It's All About

Besides a career, the search for love takes up a lot of our time. The descriptions of relationships in our world are continually changing. These changes make this topic difficult, but necessary, to study. How do we find a partner? What is the "best" relationship style?

What You Need to Know

After you read this section you should be able to:
- Understand the challenge of finding love during emerging adulthood, including defining both traditional and nontraditional approaches to relationships.
- Understand the challenges faced by gay individuals in coming out to family and friends.
- Describe the three phases in Murstein's stimulus-value-rote theory.
- Identify the factors that correlate with successful relationships and relationships that fail.
- Explain how infant attachment styles predict adult relationship experience.

Testing Your Knowledge

The objectives addressed in this section may help you solve problems or understand situations such as those presented in the questions below. At the end of this section, with the knowledge you acquire, you should be able to respond to the following questions in writing. Answer guides are given at the end of this chapter.

1. Your best friend in college has fallen desperately in love and wants guidance from you, the psychology student. What will you tell your friend about finding love?

2. Your friend Jon is gay and wants to come out to everyone in his family. Some of his family members know and have accepted him but others do not know. Based on what you've learned in this chapter, what advice can you give him?

Put It All Together

Matching Items

Match the appropriate term with its definition or description. Answers appear at the end of the chapter.

_____1. sharing the same interests with a partner

_____2. Bob and his wife agree that he will take care of child care and she will work outside the home.

_____3. successful in the world of love

_____4. dating someone because he/she is "hot"

_____5. chronically unfulfilled

_____6. never get too close

_____7. inner timetable

_____8. often involves shunning someone because he/she is gay or lesbian

_____9. no sense of an adult path

_____10. living together before marriage

A. stimulus phase
B. value-comparison phase
C. social clock
D. role confusion
E. avoidant/dismissing insecure attachment
F. secure attachment
G. cohabitation
H. homophobia
I. preoccupied/ambivalent insecure attachment
J. role phase

Multiple-Choice Questions

Circle the best answer for each question. Answers appear at the end of the chapter.

1. Emerging adulthood describes:
    A. the biological changes that occur at puberty.
    B. the life phase beginning at 18 and tapering off toward the late twenties, and being devoted to constructing an adult life.
    C. a delayed developmental period marked by lack of maturity and poor decision making.
    D. None of the above.

2. The typical role for someone experiencing emerging adulthood is:
    A. exploration of different educational or career pathways.
    B. dating.
    C. reluctance to commit.
    D. All of the above.

3. Emerging adults should conduct a targeted career search to find the right profession. This is referred to as:
   A. moratorium.
   B. foreclosure.
   C. role choice.
   D. moratorium in depth.

4. Which of the following describes a person with a biracial or multiracial identity?
   A. a person who identifies with those in same-sex relationships
   B. someone who identifies with who they are in relation to their heritage
   C. a person who has multiple identities no matter what their heritage
   D. None of the above.

5. _____ explored the challenges faced by individuals as they move from childhood into adulthood.
   A. Erik Erikson
   B. Sigmund Freud
   C. Carl Rogers
   D. Karen Horney

6. An individual with no goals or expectations for the future may be experiencing:
   A. identity diffusion.
   B. identity foreclosure.
   C. moratorium.
   D. identity achievement.

7. An individual who adopts an identity based more upon the thoughts or will of others than his/her own opinion may be experiencing:
   A. identity diffusion.
   B. identity foreclosure.
   C. moratorium.
   D. identity achievement.

8. _____ describes the healthy search for the adult self.
   A. Identity diffusion
   B. Identity foreclosure
   C. Moratorium
   D. Identity achievement

9. An individual who, after due consideration, has made a decision on a life path is experiencing:
   A. identity diffusion.
   B. identity foreclosure.
   C. moratorium.
   D. identity achievement.

10. A 35-year-old man in the United States who is just beginning his search for love would be considered:
    A. off-time.
    B. on-time.
    C. homophobic.
    D. ambivalently attached.

11. Jessie works steadily on a project for several hours, finding herself caught up in the excitement and reward of doing something she enjoys. Csikszetmihalyi would call this:
    A. task enthrallment.
    B. being in the flow.
    C. player mode.
    D. work mode.

12. Which of the following statements apply to a school-to-work transition?
    A. Employers develop relationships with some schools in Japan.
    B. This strategy is underutilized in the United States.
    C. The German apprenticeship strategy promotes this kind of transition.
    D. All of the above.

13. According to Bernard Murstein, in what order do individuals experience the mate-selection process?
    A. stimulus phase, value-comparison phase, role phase
    B. value-comparison phase, stimulus phase, role phase
    C. stimulus phase, role phase, value-comparison phase
    D. All phases take place concurrently.

14. Homogamy describes:
    A. when two people of the same sex love each other.
    B. when a person is paranoid being around lovers of the same sex.
    C. when people fall in love because of similarities in their lives.
    D. None of the above.

15. The stimulus phase of a relationship is when a couple:
    A. enter into a sexual relationship.
    B. first see each other across a crowded room.
    C. begin to work out their future together.
    D. start to talk about their shared values.

16. A person who has a preoccupied attachment style is:
    A. excessively engulfing, needy, and clingy.
    B. disengaged and standoffish.
    C. withholding and aloof.
    D. an ideal partner for genuine intimacy.

17. Clive's parents are anxious about him leaving home and going to college. Clive is getting ready to experience:
    A. adulthood.
    B. nest leaving.
    C. cohabitation.
    D. stimulus role.

Short-Answer and Essay Questions

Write a few sentences in the space below the question. For longer answers, jot down the points you want to make. Organize your ideas in an outline or other graphic method. Then, write the full essay on a separate piece of paper.

1. List and describe the four identity statuses proposed by James Marcia and compare them with those identified by Erik Erikson.

2. Describe at least three roles typical of someone experiencing emerging adulthood.

Answer Key for Chapter 10

Matching Items

1. B		6. E	
2. J		7. C	
3. F		8. H	
4. A		9. D	
5. I		10. G	

Multiple-Choice Questions

1. B	10. A
2. D	11. B
3. D	12. D
4. B	13. A
5. A	14. C
6. A	15. B
7. B	16. A
8. C	17. B
9. D	

Short-Answer and Essay Questions

1. **Question:** List and describe the four identity statuses proposed by James Marcia and compare them with those identified by Erik Erikson.

    Answer guide: Erikson first developed labels that describe the process of identity formation in adolescents: Identity confusion described those lost, drifting, or negatively shutting down; moratorium described those actively, positively seeking their identity. Marcia more carefully measured the phases that lead to identity achievement, when a person has a sense of who he is and where he's going in life. Marcia defined diffusion, foreclosure, moratorium, and achievement. Although foreclosure has negative connotations, there also are positive aspects—in particular, that there is value in emulating aspects of the lives your parents lived when you respect and admire your parents. Your answer should include all of these concepts. Did you defend the concept of achievement as a terminal position or give consideration to the idea of identity formation as continuous change?

2. **Question:** Describe at least three roles typical of someone experiencing emerging adulthood.

   Answer guide: Roles for emerging adults include student, traveler, job seeker, and mate seeker. Do not forget that we may have achievement in one area of our adult lives but not in others. Additionally, while experiencing the ups and downs of life in this phase between adolescence and adulthood, we may swing from one status to another in any of our life roles. Hopefully, in all of the roles, achievement becomes a goal that is fulfilled.

Testing Your Knowledge

Emerging Adulthood

1. **Question:** Imagine that you've made friends with an exchange student from Italy. Would your new friend view the experiences of 18- to 25-year-old Americans as similar or different to the experiences of Italians in the same age group?

   Answer guide: You are both seeking educations, love, and identity. You are roughly the same age. In the United States you may be more likely to cohabitate with your partner and your Italian friend will most likely return to Italy to live with his/her parents. Your pathway to adulthood may be more erratic.

2. **Question:** Think about your own emerging progress toward adulthood. Would you rate yourself as "adult-like" in your progress toward a committed relationship, career, financial independence? Are there differences in your levels of progress in these areas? How does this compare to the information in the textbook?

   Answer guide: Answers will vary but the important thing here is for you to reflect on your own life and to draw comparisons between your experiences and those depicted in Figure 10.1 in the text. It is common for areas of adulthood to emerge at different times and for individuals to show both progress toward and regression away from adult status.

3. **Question:** What is the social clock? In what ways are you "on-time" and in what ways are you "off-time"?

Answer guide: In your answer, you should first define the social clock. Answers for the second part of the question will vary and some things to write about are: How old were you when you graduated from high school, moved out of your parents' home, started college? Are you married? How old were you when you got married? Do you have children? How old were you when they were born? One important thing to notice is that today's social clock is much more flexible than that of 50 years ago.

Constructing an Identity

1. **Question:** You go home for vacation and your parents want to know why you haven't picked a major yet. What can you tell them about where you stand in the search for an identity? If you area member of an ethnic minority, how might this impact your search for your identity?

   Answer guide: You could be in moratorium—still actively seeking who you are and what you want to do. You could be in foreclosure—ready to take on the family business, uninterested in college. You may be in diffusion—taking in too much information to absorb, drifting without a plan. The status you have not yet reached is identity achievement in which you have a sense of who you are and where you're going in life. If you are a member of an ethnic minority you may also be grappling with developing dual identities (minority and mainstream).

Finding a Career

1. **Question:** Your friends from high school are impressed that you are now a college student. They think you must have all the right answers. They want to know if they should attend your college or if they should go to college at all. What will you tell them?

   Answer guide: There are a variety of issues that you could incorporate into your response. Did you ask your friends about the things they do that make time fly by (flow)? Are your friends workers or players—and how will that attribute make a difference in their college experience? What are their grade point averages, and what do the statistics say about individuals with those grade point averages in college?

Do their interests lie in an area that requires schooling? Do they have the economic support they need to complete college? Are they conscientious?

2. **Question:** What are some experiences that leave you with a sense of flow? Compare what you are doing in college with the information in the Interventions section "Making College a Flow Zone" in your textbook. What changes can you make?

   Answer guide: Answers will vary, but you should list experiences that make you lose all sense of time—when you become completely absorbed. Activities that provide flow might be playing music, solving a complicated math problem, or drawing, for example. In your response, you should also consider how you are immersing yourself in your college experience. Do you live on campus? Do you belong to organizations on campus? Do you attend extracurricular events? Are you connecting your classes to possible careers? Are you doing an internship or research? Making connections with your professors is also a way to maximize flow. Do you meet regularly with your advisor? Do you stay after class or take advantage of your professors' office hours? Are you trying to connect with people who are different from you? Join a club or organization outside of your normal comfort zone. There are many ways to maximize flow in your college experience.

Finding Love

1. **Question:** Your best friend in college has fallen desperately in love and wants guidance from you, the psychology student. What will you tell your friend about finding love?

   Answer guide: In your response, did you assume the friend was your sex? What if the friend was the opposite sex? Would you give the same answer? What if the other person was the same sex as your friend? Did you talk about which phase of Mursteins' theory your friend may be experiencing? Does your response incorporate the ideas of attachment styles? Does your response discuss the relevance of similarity (homogamy) issues between individuals in a couple?

2. **Question:** Your friend Jon is gay and wants to come out to everyone in his family. Some of his family members know and have accepted him, but others do not know. Based on what you've learned in this chapter, what advice can you give him?

   Answer guide: You should tell Jon that most families are accepting of their gay family members. Jon should consider his family members' religious beliefs. If they are very traditional, they may not accept him so he may not want to tell them that he is gay. Otherwise, it will be difficult, but they will more than likely accept him.

Chapter 11

Relationships and Roles

We talked about the emerging adult in the last chapter. In that chapter, we discussed some of the markers of adulthood—marriage, parenthood, and careers. These markers are interrelated. A great marriage, like a great career, would be flow inducing. Basic economic needs must be met prior to marriage or parenthood. Gender influences the roles one plays in marriage and as a parent. Society still treats males and females differently at work. Some people choose not to get married or to have children—and some women have children without being married. In some parts of the world, marriage is less relevant and polygamy still exists. In this chapter, we will discuss the adult roles of marriage, parenthood, and careers.

Marriage (pages 332–343)

What It's All About

Marriage has changed from being based on practical concerns to being based on love. Not so long ago most of us lived to be only 60-years-old, so marriages lasted approximately 40 years . . . now we often have 20 more years to live with that same person. In some areas of the world, marriage is not a goal. In the United States, it is still a major goal of adulthood. Psychologists study love and what makes it successful, and they study conflict between married couples. Although women and men in many countries spend more time sharing the roles of marriage, there are still male-dominated marriages in parts of the world. With one in every two marriages ending in divorce, psychologists study how divorce affects the couple and other family members. This section deals with many of these issues.

What You Need to Know

After you read this section you should be able to:
- Debunk some of the myths and stereotypes regarding family and work.
- Explain the main changes in the institution of marriage.
- Compare and contrast concepts of marriage across cultures.
- Debunk some of the myths and stereotypes regarding cohabitation and marriage.
- Present the U-shaped curve of marital satisfaction.
- Explain Robert Sternberg's triangular theory of love.
- Understand the importance of positive interactions between spouses.
- Present arguments for the necessity of commitment in relationship success.

- Apply insight from research on relationships to your own relationship.
- Discuss the reasons for divorce and the impact that divorce can have on marital partners, as well as on children.

Testing Your Knowledge

The objectives addressed in this section may help you solve problems or understand situations such as those presented below. At the end of this section, with the knowledge you acquire, you should be able to respond to the following in writing. Answer guides are given at the end of this chapter.

1. Many people in the United States assume that everyone wants to be married and that marriage has always been based on mutual love. Describe the evidence for or against each of these assumptions.

2. Two of your friends are getting married. Discuss what the chapter says are ways to make marriage work and what they can expect from marriage.

Parenthood (pages 344–351)

What It's All About

Do you want children? Do you have children? Some couples purposefully decide not to have children. Fertility rates in developing countries are declining, while the possibilities for parenthood have expanded significantly. More people can be parents than ever before. How do children affect a couple's life together? How do the roles of the marriage change when children arrive? Do children always make things better? Who disciplines the children and how? Who sets the rules and who has bottom-line responsibility for the family? These are a few of the questions discussed in this section.

What You Need to Know

After you read this section you should be able to:
- Describe the decline in fertility rates in the more affluent regions of the world.
- Provide arguments for and against childless marriages.
- Explain what it means to be a mother and what a mother's experience is like.
- Explain what it means to be a father and what a father's experience is like.
- Understand the impact of stress on parenting.
- Be able to give some parenting advice to future parents.

Testing Your Knowledge

The objectives addressed in this section may help you solve problems or understand situations such as that presented in the question below. At the end of this section, with the knowledge you acquire, you should be able to respond to the following question in writing. Answer guides are given at the end of this chapter.

1. A couple you know are about to become parents. Discuss the changes coming in their lives.

Work (pages 351–358)

What It's All About

The days of working for a company for life and then retiring with great benefits and a pension are over. Today U.S. employees are looking for more than simple extrinsic rewards from work. Women and men may differ in their career paths and how they view their work. Psychologists are able to help predict job satisfaction and help find the right person-job fit. This section deals with the world of work.

What You Need to Know

After you read this section you should be able to:

- Describe the many changes in the workforce, including greater work fragility and longer work hours.
- Compare and contrast the experiences of men and women in the workforce.
- Describe John Holland's six personality types that relate to occupation.
- Define the concept of career happiness and what it means to you.
- Develop some strategies for finding the ideal career.
- Consider ways in which life in a family and a society can change due to the impact of social and economic forces on workers.

Testing Your Knowledge

The objectives addressed in this section may help you solve problems or understand situations such as that presented in the question below. At the end of this section, with the knowledge you acquire, you should be able to respond to the following question in writing. Answer guides are given at the end of this chapter.

1. What can you expect from your career? Will these expectations differ depending on whether you are a man or a woman?

Put It All Together

Matching Items

Match the appropriate term with its definition or description. Answers appear at the end of the chapter.

_____1. Sternberg's theory of love
_____2. detaching marriage from social expectation
_____3. the average number of children per woman
_____4. too many demands
_____5. inner fulfillment from a job
_____6. empty marriage
_____7. torn between responsibilities
_____8. passion, intimacy, and commitment
_____9. related to marital satisfaction
_____10. happiness associated with empty nest

A. consummate love
B. triangular
C. role overload
D. intrinsic rewards
E. U-shaped curve
F. marital equity
G. commitment
H. fertility rate
I. deinstitutionalization
J. role conflict

Multiple-Choice Questions

Circle the best answer for each question. Answers appear at the end of the chapter.

1. During the late 1990s, the probability of a marriage ending in divorce was approximately:
    A. 5 percent.
    B. 14 percent.
    C. 50 percent.
    D. 75 percent.

2. _____ describes a pathological interaction where one partner presses for more intimacy or sharing and the other person tends to back off.
   A. The triangular theory of love
   B. Demand-withdrawal communication
   C. The exchange model of love
   D. The communal theory of love

3. Today, the average U.S. worker has a(n) _____ career.
   A. traditional stable
   B. boundaryless
   C. intellectually fragile
   D. esteem-challenging

4. Which of Holland's six personality types describes someone who is creative and nonconforming?
   A. social type
   B. artistic type
   C. realistic type
   D. conventional type

5. Which of Holland's six personality types describes someone who enjoys interacting with and helping others?
   A. social type
   B. artistic type
   C. realistic type
   D. conventional type

6. Someone who meets Holland's description of an entrepreneurial type might enjoy a career in:
   A. construction, appliance repair, car repair.
   B. science, research.
   C. management, sales.
   D. dance, theory, creative writing.

7. Extrinsic career rewards include:
   A. creativity and autonomy.
   B. prestige, high salary, and job security.
   C. the feeling of being connected and having opinions respected.
   D. All of the above.

8. Couples who pass this mark have passed the main danger zone for divorce.
   A. 4 years
   B. 2 years
   C. 1 year
   D. 7 years

9. Which of the following is NOT true about women and work?
   A. Women get paid less than men.
   B. Women are less educated than men.
   C. Women are more likely to move in and out of the workforce.
   D. Women may be more likely to see their work roles as secondary to their spouses'.

10. Which of the following is a characteristic of happy elderly couples?
    A. They feel each other's pain.
    B. They do not have consummate love.
    C. They engage in demand-withdrawal interactions.
    D. At least one person in the relationship has had an extramarital affair.

11. John Gottman has found that when the ratio of positive to negative interactions in a couple falls far below _____, the risk of divorce increases.
    A. 10 to 1
    B. 7 to 1
    C. 5 to 1
    D. 2 to 1

12. In order to have an enduring and happy relationship, which of the following should you NOT do?
    A. Be willing to sacrifice everything for your partner.
    B. Share exciting activities with your partner.
    C. Be predisposed to forgive your partner.
    D. Be very positive with your partner after you have been negative.

Short-Answer and Essay Question

Write a few sentences in the space below the question. For longer answers, jot down the points you want to make. Organize your ideas in an outline or other graphic method. Then, write the full essay on a separate piece of paper.

1. Discuss the concepts of career and work happiness.

Answer Key for Chapter 11

Matching Items

1.	B	6.	G
2.	I	7.	J
3.	H	8.	A
4.	C	9.	F
5.	D	10.	E

Multiple-Choice Questions

1.	C	7.	B
2.	B	8.	A
3.	B	9.	B
4.	B	10.	A
5.	A	11	C
6.	C	12.	A

Short-Answer and Essay Question

1. **Question:** Discuss the concepts of career and work happiness.
   Answer guide: Include information about Holland's personalities and how they could be used to choose careers and improve satisfaction with career choice. Discuss the person-environment fit including intrinsic and extrinsic rewards, role overload, and role conflict.

Testing Your Knowledge

Marriage

1. **Question:** Many people in the United States assume that everyone wants to be married and that marriage has always been based on mutual love. Describe the evidence for or against each of these assumptions.
   Answer guide: You should describe marriage and cohabitation trends in both the United States and Scandinavia. Also describe the dream of a married life that the majority of young people have in the United States. Regarding mutual love, you could describe arranged marriages prior to the twentieth century and the trend today toward "finding one's soul mate."

2. **Question:** Two of your friends are getting married. Discuss what the chapter says are ways to make marriage work and what they can expect from marriage.
   Answer guide: What is the chance that the marriage will end in divorce? At what point does the chance of divorce decline? You could discuss the effects of divorce since it is a real possibility. Will the wife spend her time at home or at work? Did you think about the difference that might occur in different countries and cultures? Did you discuss the U-shaped curve of happiness? What is the percentage of people who are more in love each year? Did you discuss the triangular theory of love? You should define and discuss consummate, companionate, and romantic love. You could discuss the way marriages break down. Discuss the exchange and communal models of conversation. Include the effects of flow-inducing activity and those effects on marriage. Also discuss the effects of communication styles.

Parenthood

1. **Question:** A couple you know are about to become parents. Discuss the changes coming in their lives.
   Answer guide: You can begin by discussing what your couple looks like. Are they same-sex parents or heterosexual parents? Did they adopt or have a biological child? Next, you could discuss how traditional roles in marriage become stronger when the children arrive, and whether a child will save a marriage. Include how intimacy and romance decrease, but temper that with the statistic about those who actually increase their love. Finally, you could describe the new nurturer father and the gatekeeper role of the wife.

Work

1. **Question:** What can you expect from your career? Will these expectations differ depending on whether you are a man or a woman?

Answer guide: You should describe the idea of boundaryless careers and the differences between men and women regarding their relationship to work. You can also describe strategies you can use to find your ideal career.

Chapter 12

Midlife

Middle age is easily defined as the maximum human lifespan divided by two. However, most people don't live the maximum lifespan, so maybe it should be the average lifespan divided by two. If that's the definition we want to use, should we use the average lifespan for all people in the world? That figure would not reflect the differences between countries, so maybe we should have a middle life figure for each country. But even in each country there are differences based on genetics, socioeconomic status, individual life experiences, and other factors that affect the lifespan. If we use a less mathematical approach, we could just ask people how they define middle age. We'd open up a can of worms, then! You can see it isn't easy to define middle age. For the purpose of this book we will define midlife as approximately 40 to 65 years of age.

The Evolving Self (pages 364–381)

What It's All About

Are there any changes that occur during midlife? Old wives' tales and stereotypical descriptions give us lots of conflicting views of midlife. Psychologists want a more scientific answer. Personality and intelligence are two major research areas for the time frame from the early forties to age 65. Science shows us that the Big Five personality characteristics stay basically the same, while other aspects of personality can change. As for intelligence, psychologists measure two basic types with varying results. The changes in intelligence, personality, and generativity in midlife are the focus of this section.

What You Need to Know

After you read this section you should be able to:

- Explain Belsky's statement that "middle age is a hazy, ill-defined life stage."
- Present the three contradictory views about how personality changes with age.
- Summarize the Big Five personality traits.
- Understand the concept of generativity, especially as it relates to Erikson's psychosocial stages and the research of McAdams.
- Describe the difference between hedonic and eudaimonic happiness and how they relate to generativity.
- Define and give an example of a "commitment script" and a "redemption sequence."
- Describe the standard IQ test (Wechsler Adult Intelligence Scale, or WAIS).
- Discuss the Seattle Longitudinal Study and the study of intelligence and age by K. Warner Schaie.

- Compare and contrast crystallized and fluid intelligence skills.
- Understand the important relationship between health and IQ.
- Develop ways to exercise your mind.
- Explain Paul Baltes's selective optimization with compensation theory.
- Discuss the concept of postformal thought.

Testing Your Knowledge

The objectives addressed in this section may help you solve problems or understand situations such as those presented below. At the end of this section, with the knowledge you acquire, you should be able to respond to the following in writing. Answer guides are given at the end of this chapter.

1. Describe the Big Five traits. In your answer include examples from your life or the life of someone you know to demonstrate that you understand the traits.
2. Discuss crystallized versus fluid intelligence. Define and identify similarities and differences.
3. Describe the differences between formal and postformal thinking.
4. Your parents are both in their late fifties. What things can you advise them to do so that they maintain their mental edge?

Midlife Roles and Issues (pages 382–389)

What It's All About

Many of us hope to become grandparents so we can spoil the grandchildren, then give them back to our children to deal with the consequences. Some of us become second-generation parents because our children can't handle the responsibility of parenting. The relationship we have with our children and the gender of our children flavor the grandparent experience. Because of increasing lifespans, not only do we spend time caring for our grandchildren, many of us get to care for our parents as they grow older. If you have trouble finding time for intimacy with a child in the house, imagine having your parents living with you, too. In midlife it is possible that the changes that occur in your body could make sexual activity something of the past. However, that's not a certainty! This section deals with grandparenting, parent care, and sexuality in midlife.

What You Need to Know

After you read this section you should be able to:
- Describe the many functions that grandparents play: family watchdogs, mediators, and cement.
- Understand which grandparents will be more or less involved with their grandchildren.
- Present the potential grandparent problems that might be experienced in middle adulthood.
- Understand the distress that accompanies parent care and what factors influence how people react to parent care.
- Recognize the body image issues associated with middle adulthood.
- Describe the process and outcome of menopause.
- Understand the psychological and physiological issues related to sex in middle adulthood.

Testing Your Knowledge

The objectives addressed in this section may help you solve problems or understand situations such as that presented below. At the end of this section, with the knowledge you acquire, you should be able to respond to the following in writing. Answer guides are given at the end of this chapter.

1. Describe the various roles of grandparents in the family.

Put It All Together

Matching Items

Match the appropriate term with its definition or description. Answers appear at the end of the chapter.

_____1. loss of verbal ability with sickness
_____2. cessation of ovulation and menstruation
_____3. mom or dad being cared for
_____4. the adult intelligence test
_____5. general tendency toward mental health
_____6. tendency to be risk-takers
_____7. tracked intelligence and age
_____8. basic role of grandparents
_____9. strengthens with age
_____10. a type of autobiography

A. parent care
B. commitment script
C. family watchdog
D. WAIS
E. terminal drop
F. agreeableness
G. menopause
H. neuroticism
I. openness
J. Seattle study

Multiple-Choice Questions

Circle the best answer for each question. Answers appear at the end of the chapter.

1. In their autobiographies, highly generative adults describe _____, negative events that turned out for the best.
    A. redemption sequences
    B. contamination sequences
    C. defense mechanisms
    D. boundary sequences

2. _____ refer(s) to an individual's storehouse of information accumulated over the years.
    A. Generativity
    B. Fluid intelligence
    C. Crystallized intelligence
    D. Commitment scripts

3. _____ involve(s) our ability to reason quickly when facing new intellectual challenges.
    A. Crystallized intelligence
    B. Fluid intelligence
    C. Generativity
    D. Commitment scripts

4. People whose work depends upon crystallized intelligence tend to perform best in their:
    A. twenties.
    B. thirties.
    C. fifties.
    D. sixties.

5. An individual using selective optimization with compensation to cope with losses and change experienced in later life might:
    A. focus on the most important things in life.
    B. work harder to perform well.
    C. rely on assistance to cope effectively.
    D. All of the above.

6. Postformal thinkers generally:
   A. are solution-centered.
   B. use emotional responses to compensate for the lost of intellectual acuity.
   C. thrive on considering new ideas and opinions.
   D. All of the above.

7. In describing the happiness of highly generative people, it is appropriate to say that these people are more likely to experience:
   A. hedonic happiness.
   B. eudaimonic happiness.
   C. consummate happiness.
   D. terminal happiness.

8. Twenty-year-olds tend to perform better than 60-year-olds on tasks involving:
   A. problem solving.
   B. speed.
   C. vocabulary.
   D. knowledge.

9. Which of the following is true about generativity differences between young adults and older adults?
   A. Young adults are not concerned with generativity.
   B. Older adults are only concerned with generativity related to their own families.
   C. Young adults and older adults have different priorities when it comes to generativity.
   D. There are no differences between young adults and older adults when it comes to generativity.

10. Research shows that when people reach the peak of their well-being they also show an increase in:
    A. fluid intelligence.
    B. wisdom.
    C. crystallized intelligence.
    D. openness.

Short-Answer and Essay Question

Write a few sentences in the space below the question. For longer answers, jot down the points you want to make. Organize your ideas in an outline or other graphic method. Then, write the full essay on a separate piece of paper.

1. Discuss generative and nongenerative people.

Answer Key for Chapter 12

Matching Items

1. E	6. I
2. G	7. J
3. A	8. C
4. D	9. F
5. H	10. B

Multiple-Choice Questions

1. A	6. C
2. C	7. B
3. B	8. B
4. D	9. C
5. D	10. B

Short-Answer and Essay Question

Question: Discuss generative and nongenerative people.

Answer guide: Give a definition of generativity and then discuss the concepts surrounding this Eriksonian task. Mention the difference between attitudes, activities, and priorities. How is generativity related to satisfaction? Discuss how people become generative by mentioning commitment scripts and redemption sequences. Give an example of a possible redemptive sequence in your own life or the life of a friend. Include differences psychologists find when studying various races or cultures.

Testing Your Knowledge

The Evolving Self

1. **Question:** Describe the Big Five traits. In your answer include examples from your life or the life of someone you know to demonstrate that you understand the traits.
   Answer guide: Name each of the Big Five traits. Give an example of each. For instance, my friend does not like to go to parties and is not interested in meeting new people. I enjoy parties, meeting new people, and being in crowds. My friend is introverted; I am extroverted. In your answer include characteristics of cultural influences. Also reflect on your own age and that of others you used in your answer. At what age can you expect your traits to remain fairly constant?

2. **Question:** Discuss crystallized versus fluid intelligence. Define and identify similarities and differences.
   Answer guide: Give a little history of intelligence. Follow up with definitions of crystallized and fluid intelligences. Describe the problems that exist in researching these intelligences. Next, describe the course of change in both intelligences over time. Include any activities that may help to maintain high levels of one or the other. Explain the concept of true genius and its relationship to intelligence.

3. **Question:** Describe the differences between formal and postformal thinking.
   Answer guide: Your answer should focus on three basic differences: absolute versus relative thinking, logical versus feeling-based thinking, and answer-driven versus question-driven thinking.

4. **Question:** Your parents are both in their late fifties. What things can you advise them to do so that they maintain their mental edge?
   Answer guide: Are your parents physically healthy? This has a major influence on cognitive health. Do they challenge themselves mentally? Are their jobs cognitively demanding? Do they have a mentally challenging hobby? If not, they may want to develop one to fall back on in older life. If they do have a hobby and notice that some things are more difficult now, they should consider using selective optimization with compensation. Explain to them what this is.

Midlife Roles and Issues

1. **Question:** Describe the various roles of grandparents in the family.
   Answer guide: Describe the concept of the family watchdog. Discuss how age may be a factor in grandparent attitudes. Define maternal and paternal grandparents and indicate any differences in the way families treat them. Recognize the difference between caregiving grandparents and custodial grandparents. Include data on the number of grandparent-headed households.

Chapter 13

Later Life: Cognitive and Socioemotional Development

Historians tell us that people lived for a shorter time hundreds of years ago. There were some people who had wealth and luxuries and lived into their seventies and eighties, but poor health care kept the mortality rate for the young at an extremely high level. Even today, the difference between the "haves" and "have-nots" reflects itself in longevity. The distinction today is that there are a lot more haves than ever, and even the have-nots are better off than their counterparts of 100 years ago. So, more and more people are living longer and longer lives. Society now has to cope with a large aged population that never existed in the past.

Now that we have a large population of elderly, we are noticing the effects of time on the human body. Scientists are curious about the effects of age on memory. Do we all lose our memories as we get older? Are there ways to preserve and even improve parts of memory with age? Psychologists are also interested in the changes in personality that present themselves with age. Does personality change, or does it just become more exaggerated as we get older?

In the more affluent world, we live long enough to retire. When we have worked for 50 years, longer than most of our ancestors lived, we expect—even demand—that our last 20 years be filled with leisure. In that last 20 years of life, men pass away in greater numbers than women, leaving large numbers of widows in the final years. Psychologists want to find ways for these women to survive with their mental health intact. These are some of the issues we will cover in this chapter.

Setting the Context (pages 396–398)

What It's All About

The median age of the population is increasing in many developed countries, and there may be stark contrasts between 70- and 80-year-olds. In this section, you will be introduced to the concepts of median age and the distinctions between the young-old and the old-old.

What You Need to Know

After you read this section you should be able to:

- Recognize the changing population patterns in the world (dramatic increase in the number of people age 65+).
- Explain the difference between young-old and old-old.
- Understand your own perceptions about old age.

Testing Your Knowledge

The objectives addressed in this section may help you solve problems or understand situations such as that presented in the question below. At the end of this section, with the knowledge you acquire, you should be able to respond to the following question in writing. Answer guides are given at the end of the chapter.

1. What factors have contributed to the growing median age of the U.S. population? Why is it difficult to put all older people into one category?

The Evolving Self (pages 398–409)

What It's All About

Development is a lifelong process. Some things improve, such as our knowledge base, and some things decline, such as our memory abilities. Memory declining with age is a normal part of getting older. Severe declines, such as those associated with dementia, are not a normal part of getting older. In this section, you will learn about the types of situations in which we are more likely to see memory declines, the types of memory systems that are most susceptible to decline, and some strategies that we can use to help compensate for any losses. As we move into older adulthood we also change our outlook on life. We may become more moderate in our emotional reactions to events and people—experiencing fewer and less extreme lows and highs. Using the information from the research on memory and personality can help us be happy and self-sufficient as we experience this last stage of our lifespan.

What You Need to Know

After you read this section you should be able to:
- Describe divided-attention tasks, and explain why we have difficulties with them at any age.
- Explain the information-processing perspective on memory.
- Differentiate between procedural memory, semantic memory, and episodic memory, according to the memory-systems perspective, and describe age-related changes in these memory systems.
- Develop skills to improve memory including selective optimization with compensation, using mnemonics, and improving memory self-efficacy.
- Explain the socioemotional selectivity theory.
- Describe the positivity effect.
- Discuss the upside and downside of emotional changes in middle and late adulthood.
- Explain Erikson's concept of integrity.
- Describe the types of interventions we can make to improve the mental performance of those in middle and late adulthood.

Testing Your Knowledge

The objectives addressed in this section may help you solve problems or understand situations such as those presented in the questions below. At the end of this section, with the knowledge you acquire, you should be able to respond to the following questions in writing. Answer guides are given at the end of this chapter.

1. A friend's grandmother is having problems with her memory. From the information in this section, what can you tell your friend about her grandmother's problem?

2. Based upon Carstensen's socioemotional selectivity theory, describe a typical weekend at age 20 versus a typical weekend at age 70.

Later-Life Transitions (pages 409–419)

What It's All About

Youth is wasted on the young! Just when we are retiring, our "get up and go" gets up and goes away. If we planned for our retirement, we have money to enjoy it. If not, we will begin and end retirement on the low rung of the socioeconomic ladder. Depending on our country, retirement can be very different both in economics and in health care. Men die sooner than women, leaving larger numbers of widows than widowers. This section discusses the issues of retirement and widowhood.

What You Need to Know

After you read this section you should be able to:

- Recognize the changes in the retirement age and experience of retirement in the twentieth and twenty-first centuries.
- Discuss the global differences in the experience of retirement.
- Explain the sources of income during retirement in the United States.
- Describe the special challenges that baby boomers face with retirement.
- Explain how retirement may be different for men and women.
- Describe how age discrimination can impact older adults.
- Understand social policy issues related to retirement including intergenerational equity.
- Explain the variation in reasons for retirement.
- Understand the mourning experiences of widowhood.
- Explain the factors that influence how widowed people cope.

Testing Your Knowledge

The objectives addressed in this section may help you solve problems or understand situations such as that presented in the question below. At the end of this section, with the knowledge you acquire, you should be able to respond to the following question in writing. Answer guides are given at the end of this chapter.

1. A friend's father is retiring. What can he expect from retirement?

Put It All Together

Matching Items

Match the appropriate term with its definition of description. Answers appear at the end of the chapter.

____ 1. half the population is older
____ 2. older than 79
____ 3. knowledge of how to do
____ 4. knowledge of life events
____ 5. U.S. government old-age retirement program
____ 6. saving money for retirement
____ 7. not hired because of age
____ 8. an educational/ travel program
____ 9. memorizing and monitoring
____ 10. presence of deceased spouse
____ 11. balancing needs of young and old
____ 12. over 60 compared to under 60

A.   intergenerational equity
B.   divided attention
C.   continuing bonds
D.   old-old
E.   Social Security
F.   procedural memory
G.   Elderhostel
H.   episodic memory
I.   median age
J.   age discrimination
K.   private pensions
L.   old-age dependency ratio

Multiple-Choice Questions

Circle the best answer for each question. Answers appear at the end of the chapter.

1. The positivity effect refers to:
    A. optimists living longer than pessimists.
    B. the tendency to remember positive events more than negative events.
    C. older people's tendency to focus on positive events while screening out negative ones.
    D. women being more positive than men.

2. _____ describes a subgroup of elderly who are in their sixties and seventies, typically healthy and financially secure.
    A. Young-old
    B. Old-old
    C. Senior citizen
    D. Aging young

3. _____ refers to information we automatically remember such as walking or riding a bike.
    A. Procedural memory
    B. Static memory
    C. Episodic memory
    D. Semantic memory

4. _____ refers to the fund of basic knowledge, such as who was the 16th president of the United States or what asphalt is.
    A. Procedural memory
    B. Static memory
    C. Episodic memory
    D. Semantic memory

5. _____ are words or visual imagery designed to make it easier to remember information.
    A. Mnemonics
    B. Syntaxes
    C. Semantics
    D. Imagery compensation

6. Today, a new retiree can expect to be retired for about _____ percent of their entire life.
    A. 5
    B. 15
    C. 25
    D. 30

7. In _____, the state goal is to make individuals financially comfortable during their older years, replacing roughly three-fourths of the person's working income for life.
    A. the United States
    B. Germany
    C. Hong Kong
    D. Indonesia

8. In typical situations, the U.S. Social Security system offers roughly enough income for:
    A. the basics of life.
    B. a lifestyle comparable to what the person had while working.
    C. a lavish lifestyle.
    D. a family of four.

9. Which of the following is NOT true about older workers?
    A. Retirement is an at-risk life stage.
    B. Older people are more at risk of being poor.
    C. Older workers are an at-risk group of employees.
    D. Older workers are not at risk for experiencing age discrimination.

10. Erikson's last stage of psychosocial development focuses on:
    A. integrity.
    B. generativity.
    C. stagnation.
    D. identity.

11. As we approach the end of our lives we focus on spending time with those we care about the most. This is referred to as:
    A. socioemotional selectivity.
    B. selective optimization.
    C. continuing bonds.
    D. divided attention.

12. Which of the following is the most accurate statement about widowhood mortality?
    A. Women and men are equally likely to die soon after their spouse's death.
    B. Men are more likely to die soon after their spouse's death.
    C. Women are more likely to die soon after their spouse's death.
    D. None of the above.

13. Which of the following is NOT a critical social issue related to retirement?
    A. fewer workers in relation to retirees
    B. higher poverty rates in older people
    C. reduced pension funds and savings
    D. more workers in relation to retirees

Short-Answer and Essay Question

Write a few sentences in the space below the question. For longer answers, jot down the points you want to make. Organize your ideas in an outline or other graphic method. Then, write the full essay on a separate piece of paper.

1. Discuss what we know about mourning in widows and widowers and the factors that influence coping with the loss of a spouse.

Answer Key for Chapter 13

Matching Items

1.	K	7.	J
2.	D	8.	G
3.	F	9.	B
4.	H	10.	C
5.	E	11.	A
6.	A	12.	L

Multiple-Choice Questions

1.	C	8.	B
2.	A	9.	D
3.	A	10.	A
4.	D	11.	A
5.	A	12.	B
6.	C	13.	D
7.	B		

Short-Answer and Essay Questions

1. **Question:** Discuss what we know about mourning in widows and widowers and the factors that influence coping with the loss of a spouse.

   Answer guide: Researchers ranked the loss of a spouse as one of life's most traumatic changes. It can take 2 years to associate the loss with any pleasant thoughts about the other person. Friends, children, and religion can ease the transition into single life. Did you describe the widowhood mortality effect? The gender of the survivor can make a difference. The surviving spouse's level of dependence on the other when he/she was alive can now become evident and create trouble in the new independent reality. Fortunately, this new single life can lead to emotional growth. When a widow or widower realizes that "yes, I can" attitude, the emotional growth and new thoughts about oneself can be beneficial not only mentally but physically too.

Testing Your Knowledge

Setting the Context

1. **Question:** What factors have contributed to the growing median age of the U.S. population? Why is it difficult to put all older people into one category?

   Answer guide: Your answer to the first question should focus on health care and the size of the baby boom cohort, longevity, and lower fertility rates. For the second question, your answer should focus on the distinction between the young-old and the old-old and the greater variability in development as we move into older adulthood.

The Evolving Self

1. **Question:** A friend's grandmother is having problems with her memory. From the information in this section, what can you tell your friend about her grandmother's problem?

   Answer guide: First, remember that people are selectively attuned to memory issues in the elderly. This may not be a memory issue. If she has difficulty when a task is complicated or when she must divide her attention between more than one task, it could be due to typical old age memory losses. The frontal lobe degenerates over time, and older people compensate by using more of their brain when they are thinking. This degeneration leads them to need some extra time when thinking, because they are slower, but they can eventually dig out the answer. Giving them a non-distracting environment may help too. In your answer you can discuss the three memory systems and describe the relative fragility of each. Finally, mention mnemonics as a means of improving memory, both in the young and old.

2. **Question:** Based upon Carstensen's socioemotional selectivity theory, describe a typical weekend at age 20 versus a typical weekend at age 70.
   Answer guide: Assuming that you are a healthy 20-year-old and not suffering from a terminal illness, your weekend would probably revolve around fulfilling others' expectations of you and meeting new people. As a 70-year-old, you may decide to spend the weekend working on a personal project that you enjoy or spending time with a spouse, close friend, or family members.

Later-Life Transitions

2. **Question:** A friend's father is retiring. What can he expect from retirement?
   Answer guide: In what country is this man living? Include information about the differences in retirement in specific countries. Also include the differences in retirement related to age and choice. This person is probably a baby boomer if he lives in the United States. How will this affect his retirement? If the person is on Social Security, what are the risks for poverty? What other types of retirement income might this person possess and how reliable are they? What are his hobbies or passions? This will influence how he spends his time. Suggest also the possibility of going back to work, especially to a younger retiree. Include the benefits for returning to work and discuss options as well as age discrimination in the workforce.

Chapter 14

The Physical Challenges of Old Age

Our world is going through a revolution. Although we all age, the average age should remain fairly constant, as each older person is replaced by a newborn. But that isn't happening today. People are not replacing themselves as fast as others are growing old, so the average age of the entire world population is getting older. With the large population of aged adults, we face ever-increasing challenges in adapting the world to the elderly. From ages 40 to 85 our bodies deteriorate. Our hearing, vision, muscle tone, and bone strength go downhill, picking up steam as the years increase. There is no way to know when or how far a specific person will deteriorate. Some people live very well into their old-old years. This chapter is about the physical, mental, and motor challenges facing humans as they move into old age.

Tracing Physical Aging (pages 424–430)

What It's All About

Our maximum lifespan is approximately 105 years. Our average life expectancy continues to creep closer to the maximum lifespan target. We all want to age gracefully with few troubles, living the best life we can until the end. How we age depends on genetics and the environmental interactions on our biology. You may have a predisposition toward a heart condition, but that does not mean you are predestined to die of a heart attack. Accidents, SES, ethnicity, gender, and cohort play a role in our aging process. Health care in the United States is proportioned unevenly based on the basis of SES. Although women live longer, their old age is usually frail. The risks of getting a nonfatal disease like arthritis increase greatly in the old-old years. This section discusses these topics.

What You Need to Know

After you read this section you should be able to:
- Understand the concept of "normal aging changes."
- Explain the three basic principles of age-related disease: chronic disease, activities of daily living (ADL) problems, and the defined limit of the human lifespan.
- Differentiate between instrumental ADL problems and basic ADL problems.
- Describe the socioeconomic/health gap associated with aging.
- Understand the differences in aging among the major ethnic groups of the United States: Hispanic Americans, African Americans, and Anglo Americans.
- Recognize the correlations between gender and disease, and gender and expected lifespan.

- Describe the impact of cohort and aging on health.
- Understand the importance of early health education and intervention by focusing on children and communities.

Testing Your Knowledge

The objectives addressed in this section may help you solve problems or understand situations such as that presented in the question below. At the end of this section, with the knowledge you acquire, you should be able to respond to the following question in writing. Answer guides are given at the end of this chapter.

1. Describe the process for normal aging changes that develops into disease and disability.

Sensory-Motor Changes (pages 431–438)

What It's All About

Changes occur in our visual, auditory, and motor skill abilities as we age. Some of these changes are correctable, such as by wearing glasses, contacts, or a hearing aid. Others are reversible, such as by surgery to remove cataracts or to correct near-sightedness. Other changes, such as increases in reaction time, cannot be corrected or reversed, but instead we must learn to cope with them. In this section, you will learn about the typical age-related changes in our sensory-motor systems, interventions for these changes, and how these changes create driving problems for older adults.

What You Need to Know

After you read this section you should be able to:
- Describe the age-related changes in vision.
- Learn ways to compensate for poor vision in middle and late adulthood.
- Describe how people and environments can adapt to vision loss.
- Appreciate the importance of hearing in connecting with the world.
- Understand age-related hearing loss problems (presbycusis) and implement ways to compensate for hearing loss.
- Describe changes you can make to aid those who suffer hearing loss.
- Explain age-related impairments of motor performance: slowed reaction time, osteoarthritis, and osteoporosis.
- Learn ways to improve and/or compensate for age-related motor performance.
- Discuss the debate regarding the maximum age and minimum ability requirements associated with driving privileges.

Testing Your Knowledge

The objectives addressed in this section may help you solve problems or understand situations such as that presented in the question below. At the end of this section, with the knowledge you acquire, you should be able to respond to the following question in writing. Answer guides are given at the end of this chapter.

1. Describe the typical age-related changes that may impact driving behavior in older adults. What are some ways in which older adults can cope with these problems? Think about an older adult you know and the neighborhood in which he/she lives. Is the neighborhood "friendly" for older adults who are still driving and for those who are no longer able to drive? How so? If not, what kind of changes would be needed to correct this problem?

Dementia (pages 439–444)

What It's All About

We define ourselves by our memories. The destruction of memories eventually causes the loss of the person. As we age, the probability of memory loss increases, but memory loss is not a sure thing. As with most everything else about our bodies, the environment plays a role. We should keep fit to lessen the chances of memory issues in old age. Caring for loved ones when their memory loss is significant becomes a frustrating and daunting task. This section covers many of these issues.

What You Need to Know

After you read this section you should be able to:

- Understand the difference between two primary sources of dementia: Alzheimer's disease and vascular dementia.
- Explore what is known about techniques used to detect Alzheimer's disease.
- Learn techniques, such as using external aids, to make life easier for those living with dementia.
- Learn the tips for helping people with dementia.

Testing Your Knowledge

The objectives addressed in this section may help you solve problems or understand situations such as that presented in the question below. At the end of this section, with the knowledge you acquire, you should be able to respond to the following question in writing. Answer guides are given at the end of this chapter.

1. Your grandmother has just turned 70 and has become increasingly forgetful. What signs should you look for to determine if her forgetfulness is normal or a matter of concern for her and for your family? If her condition is serious, what kinds of things can you and your family do to help her cope with her condition?

Options and Services for the Frail Elderly (pages 444–448)

What It's All About

Earth's many cultures provide numerous approaches to caring for the elderly. Recent changes in demographics and ideas of individualism are upending many traditional practices. For many reasons, the elderly tend toward poverty and need help caring for themselves. Families, community organizations, and governments are enlisted in this cause. This section describes the issues and the choices that face the elderly who can no longer care for themselves.

What You Need to Know

After you read this section you should be able to:

- Identify the wide variety of options and services for the elderly: a continuing-care retirement community, an assisted-living facility, day-care programs, home health services, nursing homes, and long-term-care facilities.
- Describe the trend toward person-oriented care but recognize potential problems in nursing home services: minimal training for certified nurse assistants and aides, low-paid employees, frequent turnover, and physically demanding work.

Testing Your Knowledge

The objectives addressed in this section may help you solve problems or understand situations such as that presented in the question below. At the end of this section, with the knowledge you acquire, you should be able to respond to the following question in writing. Answer guides are given at the end of this chapter.

1. Think about the question in the previous section. If your grandmother is just dealing with normal memory changes related to aging, what kinds of options are available for her as she begins to experience instrumental ADL problems? What if her impairments are more significant and she begins to experience basic ADL limitations? What options are there for her for these more serious limitations?

Put It All Together

Matching Items

Match the appropriate term with its definition or description. Answers appear at the end of the chapter.

_____1. long-term illnesses
_____2. difficulty performing household tasks
_____3. difficulty with basic self-care tasks
_____4. any illness producing cognitive loss
_____5. housing those with instrumental ADL
_____6. health gap between rich and poor
_____7. how some people communicate with older adults
_____8. multiple small strokes
_____9. characteristic of Alzheimer's disease
_____10. health care for the elderly

A. socioeconomic health gap
B. vascular dementia
C. dementia
D. basic ADL
E. elderspeak
F. Medicare
G. neurofibrillary tangles
H. instrumental ADL
I. chronic disease
J. assisted-living facility

Multiple-Choice Questions

Circle the best answer for each question. Answers appear at the end of the chapter.

1. ADL impairments MOST commonly become a problem during:
   A. emerging adulthood years.
   B. adulthood.
   C. young-old years.
   D. old-old years.

2. When compared with high-income individuals, low-income people are:
   A. more likely to smoke cigarettes.
   B. less likely to eat nutritious foods and exercise.
   C. more likely to work in stressful, non–flow-inducing jobs.
   D. All of the above.

3. _____ is the loss of bone density leading to bone-weakness and fracturing.
   A. Osteoporosis
   B. Presbyopia
   C. Presbycusis
   D. Arthritis

4. _____ is hearing loss caused by the atrophy of the hearing receptors located in the inner ear.
   A. Osteoporosis
   B. Presbyopia
   C. Presbycusis
   D. Arthritis

5. _____ is up-close vision loss caused by the eye's inability to focus.
   A. Osteoporosis
   B. Presbyopia
   C. Presbycusis
   D. Arthritis

6. The company where you work is providing a workshop to an older audience. What things would you suggest to the workshop coordinator to make sure the audience is well-supported?
   A. Make sure the room is well lit with dispersed, nonfluorescent lighting.
   B. Make sure course materials are available in large print.
   C. If possible, remove anything that produces a distracting background noise.
   D. All of the above.

7. Symptoms of dementia include all, EXCEPT:
   A. forgetting basic semantic information.
   B. forgetting core facts about one's life.
   C. major loss of hearing or sight.
   D. defying general social norms regarding attire or behavior.

8. _____ is a degenerative disease characterized by the loss of neurons and development of dementia.
   A. Alzheimer's disease
   B. Vascular dementia
   C. Stroke
   D. Crystallized lobes

9. Which of the following is TRUE?
   A. Women make up the majority in long-term nursing-home care.
   B. One half of United States nursing homes is ranked as "fair" or "poor" in quality.
   C. Nursing home workers often make only poverty-level wages.
   D. All of the above.

10. Which of the following is TRUE?
    A. Men tend to live longer, but women have more healthy lives.
    B. Women tend to live longer, but men have more healthy lives.
    C. Statistically, there is little difference in the average lifespan of men and women.
    D. All of the above.

11. Which of the following is NOT a normal aging change in the young-old?
    A. presbycusis
    B. dementia
    C. presbyopia
    D. increased reaction time

12. Which alternative to institutionalization is designed to provide people with the ultimate person-environment fit?
    A. continuing-care retirement community
    B. home health services
    C. assisted-living facility
    D. long-term-care facility

Short-Answer and Essay Question

Write a few sentences in the space below the question. For longer answers, jot down the points you want to make. Organize your ideas in an outline or other graphic method. Then, write the full essay on a separate piece of paper.

1. One reason why there is so much variability in how people are impacted by age is because there are many variables that affect physical challenges in old age. If you were trying to understand how a particular 75-year-old was experiencing the aging process, what would you want to know about that person and why?

Answer Key for Chapter 14

Matching Items

1.	I	6.	A
2.	H	7.	E
3.	D	8.	B
4.	C	9.	G
5.	J	10.	F

Multiple-Choice Questions

1.	D	7.	C
2.	D	8.	A
3.	A	9.	D
4.	C	10.	B
5.	B	11.	B
6.	D	12.	A

Short-Answer and Essay Question

1. **Question:** One reason why there is so much variability in how people are impacted by age is because there are many variables that affect physical challenges in old age. If you were trying to understand how a particular 75-year-old was experiencing the aging process, what would you want to know about that person and why?

   Answer guide: Your answer should address where the person lives, his or her SES level, gender, ethnicity, the presence of chronic disease, and his or her cohort.

Testing Your Knowlege

Tracing Physical Aging

1. **Question:** Describe the process for normal aging changes that develops into disease and disability.

   Answer guide: Your answer should address the three principles of age-related disease by discussing chronic disease, ADL problems, and the maximum lifespan.

Sensory-Motor Changes

1. **Question:** Describe the typical age-related changes that may impact driving behavior in older adults. What are some ways in which older adults can cope with these problems? Think about an older adult you know and the neighborhood in which he/she lives. Is the neighborhood "friendly" for older adults who are still driving and for those who are no longer able to drive? How so? If not, what kind of changes would be needed to correct this problem?

   Answer guide: Your answer should include age-related changes in vision, hearing, slowed reaction times, and the possibility of osteoporosis and osteoarthritis. Then describe ways in which these problems can be corrected or reversed. For those changes that cannot be corrected or reversed, what are some ways in which older adults can cope with the problems? In thinking about neighborhoods, did you consider the proximity of medical care facilities and shopping areas? Is there safe, reliable, and affordable public transportation? Are there services that will transport older adults to shopping and doctor's visits? Is the neighborhood well lit and how large are street signs? All of these things will impact an older adult's ability to drive or find alternative means of transportation when driving is no longer an option.

Dementia

1. **Question:** Your grandmother has just turned 70 and has become increasingly forgetful. What signs should you look for to determine if her forgetfulness is normal or a matter of concern for her and for your family? If her condition is serious, what kinds of things can you and your family do to help her cope with her condition?

   Answer guide: Your answer should include the symptoms of dementia. Since your grandmother is only 70, it is not very likely that she is suffering from the beginning of dementia. However, if she is, then you would need to consider whether she has had some small strokes or has Alzheimer's disease. You would want her to be evaluated by a professional. If she has dementia, then you should list the things you and your family can do to make her life predictable and safe.

Options and Services for the Frail Elderly

1. **Question:** Think about the question in the previous section. If your grandmother is just dealing with normal memory changes related to aging, what kinds of options are available for her as she begins to experience instrumental ADL problems? What if her impairments are more significant and she begins to experience basic ADL limitations? What options are there for her for these more serious limitations?

   Answer guide: For instrumental ADL problems, you should describe home health services and the possibility of a continuing-care retirement community. For more basic ADL problems, you should describe the benefits of assisted living and the possibility of day care and nursing homes or long-term-care facilities for more severe impairments.

Chapter 15

Death and Dying

In our final view of human development, we discuss the effects of death on survivors and the issues surrounding dying. We usually don't know when death will occur: today, tomorrow, or next year. We can predict the general life expectancy, and if nothing untoward occurs, we each can expect a general number of years in a full lifetime. Our lifespan depends on many variables, including our country's economic condition, our family's socioeconomic status, our biology defined by our ancestry, and our access to medical care. Most of us want to be in control of our death to make it as comfortable as possible. But cultures differ in how death is understood and the ways people cope with death. This chapter discusses many of these issues.

Setting the Context (page 456)

What It's All About

Death can follow one of several pathways. In affluent countries, like the United States, death usually follows a long and erratic trajectory.

What You Need to Know

After you read this section you should be able to:
- Understand the three pathways to death: (1) death occurs suddenly, (2) death occurs after a steady decline in health, and (3) death occurs after a long and difficult struggle, typically due to illness.

Testing Your Knowledge

The objectives addressed in this section may help you solve problems or understand situations such as that presented in the question below. At the end of this section, with the knowledge you acquire, you should be able to respond to the following question in writing. Answer guides are given at the end of the chapter.

1. How might someone view death?

A Short History of Death (pages 456–458)

What It's All About

Our views of death are influenced by the time and place in which we live. Death in the Western world used to be viewed as a natural, everyday occurrence, and everyone was exposed to death. When medical science began to understand diseases, the dead and the dying were secluded from the living, and as medical science has continued to advance, the exclusion of the dying continues with most people dying in the hospital. Not all cultures have the same view of death, and you will be introduced to these differences in this section and learn about the historical view of death in the United States.

What You Need to Know

After you read this section you should be able to:

- Become familiar with the historical and cultural approaches to handling death and dying.

Testing Your Knowledge

The objectives addressed in this section may help you solve problems or understand situations such as that presented in the question below. At the end of this section, with the knowledge you acquire, you should be able to respond to the following question in writing. Answer guides are given at the end of the chapter.

1. Can you think of people you know or know of who fit one of the three pathways to death? Describe the circumstances of their deaths.

The Dying Person (pages 458–465)

What It's All About

Social scientists study different aspects of death. Elisabeth Kübler-Ross may have the most famous theory on the emotional adjustments we make when we are faced with our imminent death—though, as you will see in this chapter, there is controversy surrounding her theory. We all want to die well, but each of us has a different definition of what "well" means. Certainly, an untimely death would not be considered a good death. This section discusses some of these issues.

What You Need to Know

After you read this section you should be able to:

- Explain Kübler-Ross's stages of dying: denial, anger, bargaining, depression, and acceptance.
- List and explain the criticisms of Kübler-Ross's stage theory.
- Recognize that people who are dying tend to behave just as they did when they were living their lives.
- Understand the fact that some people want to know they are dying and others do not. Everyone responds to death in his or her own unique way.
- Describe the different emotions expressed by someone who is dying, including the concept of middle knowledge.
- Understand that it is harder to accept a death, like the death of a child, that has happened "off-time" in terms of our social clock.
- Explain the concept of a "good death."

Testing Your Knowledge

The objectives addressed in this section may help you solve problems or understand situations such as those presented in the questions below. At the end of this section, with the knowledge you acquire, you should be able to respond to the following questions in writing. Answer guides are given at the end of this chapter.

1. A fellow student has been told he has 6 months to live. According to this section, what would you expect him to do?

2. What can health-care professionals do to help parents who have a terminally ill child, both before and after the child's death?

The Health-Care System (pages 465–471)

What It's All About

Where would you like to die? Some of us would prefer to die in our own beds in our own homes surrounded by our loved ones. A few of us get that chance, but others die in hospitals or in nursing homes. Who gets to decide the type of care we will receive in the last months or days of our lives? How caring will that care be? The answers to these questions depend on your SES, the training given to your health-care professionals, the disease from which you are suffering, and the directives you left in case you are incapacitated.

What You Need to Know

After you read this section you should be able to:

*   Describe the shortcomings of traditional hospital care for the dying.
*   Explain the "dying trajectory" and the effect it has on the quality of care provided by hospital staff.
*   Know that "end-of-life care instruction" should be a component of every health-care professional's training.
*   Understand the role of palliative care services at a traditional hospital.
*   Describe the pros and cons of hospice care in the natural death process.
*   Explain the reasons why some people want to die at home, while others want to die in the hospital or hospice facility.

Testing Your Knowledge

The objectives addressed in this section may help you solve problems or understand situations such as that presented in the question below. At the end of this section, with the knowledge you acquire, you should be able to respond to the following question in writing. Answer guides are given at the end of this chapter.

1. From the previous question, what will be the likely alternatives for this student's care as he progresses toward his untimely death?

The Dying Person: Taking Control of How We Die (Pages 472–476)

What It's All About

Death is a frightening topic for many of us. Perhaps this is because of our inability to control so many things related to it. We do have some control, however, in our ability to have a "good death." In this section, you will learn about the different types of advance directives that you can create to provide instructions about your death. You will also learn about the controversial topics of euthanasia, physician-assisted suicide, and age-based rationing of care.

What You Need to Know

After you read this section you should be able to:

- Take steps to prepare for the end of life, and describe the following advanced directives: living will, durable power of attorney for health care, Do Not Resuscitate (DNR) order, and Do Not Hospitalize (DNH) order.
- Discuss the controversial topics of passive euthanasia, active euthanasia, and physician-assisted suicide.
- Describe the controversial issue of age-based rationing of care.

Testing Your Knowledge

The objectives addressed in this section may help you solve problems or understand situations such as that presented in the question below. At the end of this section, with the knowledge you acquire, you should be able to respond to the following question in writing. Answer guides are given at the end of this chapter.

1. Again following your classmate: How would you expand on the care instructions that he may use to take some control of his death?

Put It All Together

Matching Items

Match the appropriate term with its definition or description. Answers appear at the end of the chapter

_____1. terminally ill people go through five stages

_____2. not understanding your imminent death

_____3. projecting the pathway to death

_____4. promoting dignified dying

_____5. providing palliative care at home

_____6. stating wishes to control your care

_____7. in a medical crisis, do not hospitalize

_____8. withholding medical treatment for the old-old

_____9. the study of death and dying

_____10. taking action to help a person die

A. living will
B. age-based rationing of care
C. thanatology
D. middle knowledge
E. dying trajectory
F. Kübler-Ross's theory
G. DNH
H. active euthanasia
I. hospice movement
J. palliative care

Multiple-Choice Questions

Circle the best answer for each question. Answers appear at the end of the chapter.

1. A "good death" is one characterized by:
   A. the feeling one had achieved a purpose in life.
   B. freedom from debilitating pain.
   C. the feeling of control over how one dies.
   D. All of the above.

2. Care outside the home designed to provide comfort to a patient and relieve symptoms rather than provide a cure is called:
    A. hospice care.
    B. palliative care.
    C. resuscitative measures.
    D. curative care.

3. At-home care designed to provide comfort to a patient and relieve symptoms rather than provide a cure is called:
    A. hospice care.
    B. palliative care.
    C. resuscitative measures.
    D. curative care.

4. Barriers to hospice care include:
    A. an unwillingness on the part of the individual to accept impending death.
    B. the burden on family members of providing daily care to the patient at home until death comes.
    C. reluctance of physicians and family members to approach the terminally ill and take away their last hope.
    D. All of the above.

5. Which of the following are forms of advance directives?
    A. a living will
    B. a durable power of attorney for health care
    C. a DNR order
    D. All of the above.

6. _____ is a legal form of euthanasia in which potentially life-saving treatments such as a feeding tube are withheld.
    A. Passive euthanasia
    B. Active euthanasia
    C. Involuntary euthanasia
    D. Physician-assisted suicide

7. _____ is a legal form of euthanasia in which a health-care professional gives a patient a means of ending his or her own life.
    A. Passive euthanasia
    B. Active euthanasia
    C. Involuntary euthanasia
    D. Physician-assisted suicide

8. A _____ is a document filled out by a doctor in consultation with the patient's family. It stipulates that if cardiac arrest takes place, health-care professionals should NOT try to revive the patient.
    A. living will
    B. durable power of attorney for health care
    C. Do Not Resuscitate order (DNR)
    D. euthanasia order

9. A _____ is a document filled out by the patient and his or her lawyer giving another person decision-making authority if the patient is not able to make his or her own decisions.
    A. living will
    B. durable power of attorney for health care
    C. Do Not Resuscitate order (DNR)
    D. euthanasia order

Short-Answer and Essay Question

Write a few sentences in the space below the question. For longer answers, jot down the points you want to make. Organize your ideas in an outline or other graphic method. Then, write the full essay on a separate piece of paper.

1. Discuss the issues surrounding euthanasia and physician-assisted suicide.

Answer Key for Chapter 15

Matching Items

1. F
2. D
3. E
4. J
5. I
6. A
7. G
8. B
9. C
10. H

Multiple-Choice Questions

1. D
2. B
3. A
4. D
5. D
6. A
7. D
8. C
9. B

Short-Answer and Essay Question

1. **Question:** Discuss the issues surrounding euthanasia and physician-assisted suicide.
   Answer guide: Define each of the following terms in your essay: passive euthanasia; active euthanasia; physician-assisted suicide. Give examples where any of these are legalized procedures. Check the Internet for the latest statistics on the use of passive euthanasia and physician-assisted suicide. Maybe look up the court rulings and use them in your essay. An idea: Take a stance, either pro or con, and find another student with the opposite position. Write your papers together in the form of a debate.

Testing Your Knowledge

Setting the Context

1. **Question:** How might someone view death?
   Answer guide: In what era did this person live? Views of death were different in the Middle Ages when compared to the eighteenth and nineteenth centuries. Today's views are also different from previous centuries. Did you discuss the person's culture?

A Short History of Death

1. **Question:** Can you think of people you know or know of who fit one of the three pathways to death? Describe the circumstances of their deaths.
   Answer guide: Answers will vary but an example of Pathway 1 should include the death of someone who died unexpectedly. Pathway 2 should include someone who was diagnosed with an advanced condition and steadily declined. Pathway 3 should include the death of someone who had periods of being ill and then getting better but eventually succumbed to the illness.

The Dying Person

1. **Question:** A fellow student has been told he has 6 months to live. According to this section, what would you expect him to do?
   Answer guide: Kübler-Ross thought he would go through five stages. Did you name those in your answer? Today we think a little differently. Your friend may or may not go through those stages, and he may not go through them in order. In the past, we would force patients to "discuss" their impending death. Today we know that it isn't a good idea to force people to talk about it, if they aren't ready. Did you include the cultural differences in expressions in your answer? You should also include the concept of middle knowledge in your answer. In some cases, the patient may get energized. So, it is hard to generalize a pattern of behavior. Did you talk about the parents of this student and their reactions?

2. **Question:** What can health-care professionals do to help parents who have a terminally ill child, both before and after the child's death?
   Answer guide: Be sure to discuss the things that can be done before the child dies—discuss the possibility of death and invite parents to be involved in the child's care. After the child's death, health-care professionals can attend the funeral

or memorial service, write letters of condolence, and listen to people's stories.

The Health Care System

1. **Question:** From the previous question, what will be the likely alternatives for this student's care as he progresses toward his untimely death?

   Answer guide: Discuss the problems associated with hospital care and weigh that against the necessity for health-care professional access. Mention the dying trajectory and how human nature includes a need to predict the pathway of death. Remember that predictable deaths are thought of as "good," while those that do not follow the assumed pattern are considered "bad" deaths. Discuss palliative care and the instructions that patients can leave the hospital staff. Outside the hospital a person can choose to be home in hospice. Describe hospice and the cultural issues involved in taking advantage of this type of care. In your answer, include statistics on the amount of time people spend in hospice.

The Dying Person: Taking Control of How We Die

1. **Question:** Again following your classmate: How would you expand on the care instructions that he may use to take some control of his death?

   Answer guide: This question is all about the advanced directives that are available to us through the law. There are living wills, but they are mostly used by people of specific SES. Did you include that information in your answer? You should describe the DNR, DNH, and the power of attorney for health care. Finally you should also discuss the concepts surrounding ending one's life. Which are legal? Which are not? What are differences among countries?